SQL

- A SIMPLE INTRODUCTION BY CLIFF

SQL BEGINNINGS

CLIFF BEACHAM

outskirtspress
DENVER, COLORADO

The opinions expressed in this manuscript are solely the opinions of the author and do not represent the opinions or thoughts of the publisher. The author has represented and warranted full ownership and/or legal right to publish all the materials in this book.

SQL- a Simple Introduction by Cliff
SQL Beginnings
All Rights Reserved.
Copyright © 2014 Cliff Beacham
v2.0

Cover Photo © 2014 Cliff Beacham. All rights reserved - used with permission.

This book may not be reproduced, transmitted, or stored in whole or in part by any means, including graphic, electronic, or mechanical without the express written consent of the publisher except in the case of brief quotations embodied in critical articles and reviews.

Outskirts Press, Inc.
http://www.outskirtspress.com

ISBN: 978-1-4787-2450-6

Outskirts Press and the "OP" logo are trademarks belonging to Outskirts Press, Inc.

PRINTED IN THE UNITED STATES OF AMERICA

Cliff's™ SQL Server Workshops: Querying SQL Server by Cliff Beacham

Copyright © Cliff Beacham 1998, 2007, 2012. All rights reserved.
Printed in the United States of America.

Published by Cliff Beacham Inc., 4621 E Colorado St, Long Beach, CA 90814.
This book may also be purchased for educational, business, or sales promotional use. Online editions are also available for most titles in the series.

    Editor: Cliff Beacham
    Production Editor: Cliff Beacham
    Copyeditor: Cliff Beacham
    Proofreader: Cliff Beacham
    Indexer: Cliff Beacham
    Cover Designer: Cliff Beacham
    Interior Designer: Cliff Beacham
    Illustrators: Cliff Beacham

Printing History:
    March 1998: First Edition.
    June 2007: Second Edition.
    January 2014: Third Edition.

Trademarks:
Many of the designations used by manufacturers and sellers to distinguish their products are claimed as trademarks. Where those designations appear in this book, and Cliff Beacham, Inc. was aware of a trademark claim, the designations have been printed in caps or initial caps.

Errors and Omissions:
While every precaution has been taken in the preparation of this book, the publisher and author assumes no responsibility for errors or omissions, or for damages resulting from the use of the information contained herein.

Small print:
The technologies discussed in this publication, the limitations on these technologies that technology and content owners seek to impose, and the laws actually limiting the use of these technologies are constantly changing. Thus, some of the code examples described in this publication may not work, may cause unintended harm to systems on which they are used, or may not be consistent with applicable user agreements.
Your use of these examples is at your own risk, and Cliff Beacham, Inc. disclaims responsibility for any damage or expense resulting from their use. In any event, you should take care that your use of these examples does not violate any applicable laws, including copyright laws.

This book uses a durable and flexible lay-flat binding.

ISBN-10: 0-000-00000-5
ISBN-13: 000-0-000-00000-8

Introduction and Overview

Whenever any study is undertaken, no matter what the subject, it is an advantage for a reader to establish a framework to place topics in context.

A table of contents gives chapter headings and will be some use in this regard but the recognized training technique of telling students what you are going to tell them, then telling them and then telling them what you have just told them is very useful for placing content in context.

Books of 1000 pages and more have been written about the subjects contained in this book but my aim is to keep it as brief as possible but still cover the material which is the basis for getting started with the subject of SQL queries in Microsoft™ SQL Server. Please feel free to pass your comments to me regarding the success of this endeavor.

The book starts with an examination of the design of a database (briefly) by looking at the Relational model, Normalization and Schemas. This chapter is intended to provide an introduction to the storage of data - it is needed in order to understand the context of the other chapters. It is not meant to supply all the facts about relational storage but probably no book could ever hope to address all there is to know about relational theory. The objective is to introduce the reader to how data is stuctured for storage in tables.

Next the components of a SQL Server database is discussed to widen the reader's understanding of structure from mere tables to include datatypes, constraints, internal programs called stored procedures and triggers and indexes. Also tables that can be created, dropped and/or altered.

The third chapter starts to look at the basic SELECT statement and starts providing real-world examples of queries. It introduces the anatomy of the T-SQL SELECT statement and then discusses how to choose what data you want to retrieve.

Chapter 4 moves beyond the basics to expressions, operators and functions. Then discusses some more advanced code that filters data according to a defined resultset.

It may seem that chapter 5 is misplaced – being a chapter on Tips but it is here deliberately – at a point where the reader can understand the issues and start to benefit from doing it right first time round.

Retrieving (querying) data is continued with an advanced discussion covering the situations of more than one table (JOINS), nesting queries (SUBQUERIES) using tables to receive data and as intermediate temporary tables (SELECT INTO) and combing results of queries with the UNION operator.

In Chapter 7 the subject is Modifying data i.e. INSERT, UPDATE and DELETE.

Views are nothing more than stored queries and are examined in Chapter 8. A view may be thought of as another way of viewing the data, usually from multiple tables. The chapter discusses creating views, modifying data through views and the advantages that can be gained by this approach.

Data Integrity is a section that covers the topics that ensures the accuracy and reliability of the data. The integrity of the database is guaranteed by the implementation of Entity Integrity, Domain Integrity and Referential integrity. These objectives are met by using the techniques covered in Chapter 9, Defaults, Rules, and Constraints. Constraints are defined, the different types of constraints and when it is appropriate to use each type. The purpose and implementation of the identity property is also discussed.

Chapter 10 is a description of stored procedures, how to create them and some rules and guidelines. The section includes the use of parameters, obtaining output from a stored procedure and executing a stored procedure. Also the use of an execution plan and the recompile option.

Triggers are an advanced form of rule which are bound to a table. Chapter 11 discusses the basic 3 types of triggers, their creation and offers some guidelines. How triggers work is described and how they can be used to enforce data integrity. Also Multi-row triggers, business rules and other considerations are introduced. The chapter does not go into great depth but stops at the introductory level.

Chapter 12 introduces Indexes. There is nothing that affects performance like indexes. This chapter covers the different types of indexes, their rules, where each type should be used and performance considerations, optimizer hints statistics, fillfactor, sorting and data fragmentation.

Batches and scripts are discussed in Chapter 13. Then Transaction management including locks on data and transaction rollback.

The final chapter (14) discusses Control-of-flow language which includes a discussion of variables, error raising, case statements, loops and blocks and, finally, the execute statement.
Cursors are then covered: declaring, opening, closing, the fetch statement, when to use them and when not to use them.

All in all this book is an <u>introduction</u> to querying SQL Server. More advanced discussions can build upon the foundation laid here. A comment from a friend of mine comes to mind. It will take you two weeks to learn SQL and two years to get good at it.

Querying SQL Server databases

Contents

Introduction and Overview 1
Chapter 1 - Database Design 1
  1   Data, Design and Normalization 5
  1A Some definitions 5
  1B Database Design 7
    1B.1 Hierarchical design model - one-to-many 9
    1B.2 Network design model - many-to-many 10
    1B.3 Relational design model - passive independent data 10
    1B.4 Database Design Considerations 12
  1C Normalization 13
    1C.1 The First Normal Form 14
    1C.2 The Second Normal Form 15
    1C.3 The Third Normal Form 17
    1C.4 Benefits of Normalization 18
  1D Denormalization 19
  1E Some suggestions for normalized design 20
  1F The ERA Model 23
    1F.1 Entities 23
    1F.2 Relationships 24
    1F.2a   one-to-one (1:1) 24
    1F.2b   one-to-many (1:n) 24
    1F.2c   many-to-many (n:m) 24
  1G Keys 25
    1G.1 Primary Keys (PK) 25
    1G.2 Foreign Keys (FK) 25
  1H Attributes 26
  1I Modeling Elements 27
  1J The Schema 27

Chapter 2 – Database Objects 3

2A Database Components 5
2A.1 User Databases 5
2A.1a The pubs sample database 5
Exercise: 5
Exercise: 5
2A.1b The Northwind sample database (the MS Access sample database) 6
Exercise: 6
2B   Database Components 7
2B.1   Database Objects 7
2B.2   Indexes (type sp_helpindex *tablename*) 8
2B.3   Datatypes (type SELECT * FROM systypes) 8
2B.4   Constraints (type sp_help constraints) 8
2C   System Stored Procedures 9
2D   Creating Tables 11
2D.1   Datatypes 11
2D.2   System supplied Datatypes 12
2D.3   NULL 13
2D.4   User defined Datatypes 14
2D.5   Special Datatypes 16
2D.6   Exact and Approximate Numeric Data 17
2D.7   Adding and Dropping Datatypes 18
2E   The CREATE TABLE statement 19
2E.1   Temporary Tables 20
2E.2   The DROP TABLE statement 20
2B.3   The ALTER TABLE statement 20

Chapter 3 - SELECT 1
3   The Select Statement 5
3A   SELECT 8
3A.1   * 10
3A.2   a list of column names 10
3A.3   column names and column headings 12
3A.4   an expression 13
3A.5   the IDENTITYCOL keyword (instead of the name of the column) 14
3A.6   global variables 15
3A.7   a local variable assignment 16
3A.8   a literal enclosed in quotes 16
3A.9   a nested subquery 16
3A.10 What not to do - Cartesian Product 17
3B   INTO 18
3C   FROM 19
3D   WHERE 20
3E   GROUP BY 21
3E.1   Cube and Rollup (These are super aggregates) 22
3F   HAVING 23
3G   ORDER BY 24
3H   COMPUTE 26

Chapter 4 - SELECT Plus 1
4   Expressions, Operators, Functions 5
4A   Expressions 5
4A.1 Constants and Variables 7
4A.2 Operators 8
4A.3 Functions 17
4A.3a   Numeric Functions 17
4A.3a.1   Numeric Mathematical Functions 17
4A.3a.2   Numeric Aggregate Functions 19
4A.3b   String Functions (or Character functions) 22
4A.3c   Datetime Data 24
4A.3d   System Functions 26
4A.3d.1   System tables 26
4A.3d.2   Niladic Functions 27
4A.3e   Datatype Conversion 28
4A.3f   Text and Image Functions 29

4B	Choosing Rows	30
4B.1	Example based on a comparison:	31
4B.2	Example based on a range (BETWEEN):	31
4A.3	Example based on a list (IN):	32
4B.4	Example based on a character string (LIKE):	32
4B.5	Example based on unknown Values	34
4B.6	Example based on several arguments	34
4B.7	Negations	35
4B.8	Eliminating duplicates (DISTINCT)	36

Chapter 5 - Tips 1

5.1	Start with Use DB	5
5.2	Highlight code and execute	5
5.3	Comment-bracket subsidiary code in the window pane	5
5.4	Copy/Paste – don't type names	5
5.5	Build-up queries	6
5.6	Query results to Grid, File, Text and why	6
5.7	Save query code to File>>Save SQL query as	6
5.8	Develop a Style	6
5.9	F5	7
5.10	Copy result set to clipboard	7
5.11	Run a harmless query before DML	7
5.12	Establish a war-chest of your own	7
5.13	Learn to search the iNet	8
5.14	Don't play in the ProdDB	8
5.15	Backup according to a plan and test restores	8
5.16	Start View and SP names with a number to top list them	8
5.17	Always write comments in your SPs	8
5.18	Use a naming convention	10
5.19	Use intuitive names – avoid abbreviations but don't get rediculous	10
5.20	Set Tools>>Options	11
5.21	Alter you recent file to Max which is 24	11
5.22	Set up a folder for your query results – expand to a folder structure	11
5.23	Use Query Option = Results to Text to list your Column names	12
5.24	Use WHERE 1 = 2 to get headings only	12
5.25	Learn shortcuts	13
5.26	Include Statistics if you want to tune your query	13
5.27	Intellisense	13

5.28	Copy with headers	13
5.29	Niladic functions	13
5.30	Use Environment\Keyboard to set you own shortcuts	15
5.31	When writing SPs use a DROP statement commented out	15
5.32	Intelligent aliases in code not a b etc	15
5.33	Consider including DB name in result sets	15
5.34	Don't BU to tape	16
5.35	Establish BU plan ASAP	16
5.36	Copy 2xClk Word	16
5.37	Start selection item with a , (Comma)	16
5.38	Learn to Detach and Attach DB's	17
5.39	Copy a Name from the Object Explorer pane	17
5.40	Get the name of the server	17
5.41	Develop your own techniques for enhancing readability	17
5.42	Write a UDF (User-defined Function)	18
5.43	What makes DateTime so difficult and complex?	19
5.44	Using Table Aliases	21
5.45	Use a harmless query before a DML statement	22

Chapter 6 - Joins 1

6A	JOIN	5
6A.1	The Rules:	6
6A.2	Unrestricted JOINS (a.k.a. Cross Join)	7
6A.3	Equijoins	8
6A.4	Natural Joins	8
6A.5	JOINS with more than two tables	9
	6A.5a Aliasing table names in JOINS	11
	6A.5b Adding a filter (WHERE) when you use JOIN syntax	12
6A.6	Self joins (joins within one table)	13
6A.7	Outer joins	15
	6A.7a Using NULL in search conditions	17
6A.8	Theta join	17
6B	SUBQUERIES	18
6B.1	Nesting SELECT statements	21
6B.2	3 Types of subquery	21
	6B.2a with comparison operators	21
	6B.2b with the IN clause	22
	6B.2c with the EXISTS clause	23
6B.3	Subquery restrictions/rules	24

6B.4 Correlated subqueries	26
6C SELECT INTO statement	27
6D UNION operator	28

Chapter 7 – Modifying Data 1

7A INSERTING ROWS	5
7A.1 The INSERT statement	5
7A.1a Default options	7
7A.1b INDENTITY keyword	8
7A.1c Inserting partial data	9
7A.2 INSERT SELECT (Inserting multiple rows)	11
7A.3 INSERT EXEC	13
7A.4 INSERT . . . . INTO	14
7B UPDATING ROW DATA	16
7B.1 The UPDATE statement	16
7B.2 Updating based on data from other tables	18
7C DELETING ROWS	19
7C.1 The DELETE statement	19
7C.2 Removing rows based on data from other tables	21

Chapter 8 - Views 5

8A What is a View?	5
8B Advantages of views:	6
8B.1 View considerations	7
8C Creating Views	8
Dropping Views	10
8D View information	10
8E View options	11
8E.1 "WITH CHECK" option	11
8E.2 "WITH ENCRYPTION" option	12
8F Projection example	12
8G Join example	13
8H A view of a view example	14
8I Computed column example	14
8J Aggregate functions example	15
8K Modifying data through views	16
8L Modifications to tables with NOT NULL columns	17
8M Views as security mechanisms	17

Chapter 9 - Data Integrity 1
9A Data Integrity 4
9A.1 What is Data Integrity? 4
    9B.1   Entity Integrity (Row restrictions) 5
    9B.2   Domain Integrity (Column restrictions) 6
    9B.3   Referential Integrity (restrictions based on columns in other tables) ... 7
    9B.4   User defined 7
9A.3 Enforcing Data Integrity 8
    9C.1   Procedural Data Integrity 8
    9C.2   Declarative Data Integrity 8
9B IDENTITY property/attribute 9
9B.1 Using IDENTITY columns 10
9C Creating and Implementing Defaults and Rules 12
    DEFAULTS 12
    RULES 13
9C.1 Using Defaults to Enforce Data Integrity 13
9C.2 Using Rules to Enforce Data Integrity 14
9C.3 Binding Defaults and Rules 15
9C.4 Unbinding and Dropping Defaults and Rules 16
9D Using Constraints to Enforce Data Integrity 18
9D.1 Defining Constraints (and Dropping) 20
9D.2 Implementing Constraints 21
9D.3 Types of Constraint 23
    9D.3a.1   Unique constraints 23
    9D.3a.2   Primary key constraints 24
    9D.3b.1   CHECK type constraints 26
    9D.3b.2   DEFAULTS (2 types) 28
    9D.3c   Foreign Key Constraint (REFERENCES Constraint) 30
4D.4 When to use Data Integrity Constraints 32
4D.5 Examples of CREATE TABLE statements 34

Chapter 10 – Stored Procedures 1
1 What is a Stored Procedure? 3
    1A   Using Stored Procedures 4
    1B   Benefits of using Stored procedures 5
    1C   Stored Procedures are independent 5

2 Creating a Stored Procedure 7
    2A   Dropping a Stored Procedure 7
    Running a Stored Procedure 8
    Dropping a Stored Procedure 9

3   Rules and Guidelines 10
4   Parameters 11

Chapter 11 - Triggers 1
1   What is a trigger? 4
2   Creating and Dropping a trigger 6
3   Trigger Rules and guidelines 7
4   Modification Triggers 8
    4A   INSERT trigger 9
    4B   DELETE triggers 11
    4C   UPDATE Triggers 12
    4D   AFTER Triggers 14
    4E   INSTEAD OF Triggers 16

5   Enforcing integrity with triggers 17
    5A   Enforcing data integrity 17
    5B   Enforcing Referential integrity 18

6   Multi row trigger 20
7   Business rules 21
8   Getting Information about Triggers 22

Chapter 12 – Indexes 1

12.1 IMPLEMENTING INDEXES 7
- 12.1A   Reasons for using Indexes 7
- 12.1B   Reasons for not Indexing 8
- 12.1C   Initial Guidelines for Indexing Columns 9
- 12.1D   Columns that should not be Indexed 9

12.2 Creating an Index 10
- 12.2A   Some Index Rules 10
- 12.2B   Duplicate rows and keys 11

12.3 Types of Indexes 13
- 12.3A   Clustered Indexes 13
- 12.3B   Nonclustered Indexes 16

12.4 Characteristics of Indexes 18
- 12.4A   Unique Indexes 18
- 12.4B   Composite Indexes 19

12.5 Performance Considerations 20
- 12.5A   Index Usage 20
- 12.5B   Optimizer Hints 27
- 12.5C   The UPDATE STATISTICS command 28
- 12.5D   Query Covering 29
- 12.5E   FILLFACTOR 31
- 12.5F   SORTED_DATA & SORTED_DATA_REORG 33
- 12.5G   DBCC SHOWCONTIG 34

Chapter 13 – Scripts and Transactions 1

13.1 Batches and Scripts 4
- 13.1A   Scripts 4
- 13.1B   Batches 4
- 13.1C   Combining Statements in a single batch 5
- 13.1D   Batch Rules 6
- 13.1E   Invalid Batch Examples 7

13.2 Transaction Management 8
- 13.2A   Processing - ATOMICITY 8
- 13.2B   Database Consistency and Concurrency 9
- 13.2C   Locks 9
- 13.2C.1   Types of Lock 9
- 13.2C.1a   Shared Locks 9
- 13.2C.1b   Update Locks 9
- 13.2C.1c   Exclusive Locks 10

13.2C.2	What can be locked by SQL Server	11
13.2C.3	Lock Escalation	12
13.2C.4	Locking Options	13
13.2C.4a	Row Level Locking	15
13.2D	Transactions	16
13.2D.1	A Transaction is a Unit of Work and a Unit of Recovery	16
13.2D.2	User defined Transactions	17
13.2D.3	Rollback Transaction	19
13.2D.4	SAVEPOINT	20

Chapter 14: Programming 3

14.1 Control of Program Flow Language 4

14.1A	DECLARE	4
14.1A.1	Local Variables	5
14.1A.2	Global Variables	6
14.1B	RETURN	7
14.1C	RAISERROR	8
14.1D	PRINT	11
14.1E	CASE	12
14.1F	BEGIN . . . . END Block	15
14.1G	IF . . . . ELSE Block	16
14.1H	WHILE construct	17
14.1I	EXECUTE	18
14.1J	WAIT FOR	21

2   Cursors 22

14.2A	ANSI Cursors	23
14.2B	Enhanced SQL Engine Cursors	23
14.2C	ANSI SQL Cursors	23
14.2C.1	DECLARE statement	25
14.2C.2	OPEN statement	26
14.2C.3	FETCH statement	27
14.2C.4	CLOSE statement	28
14.2C.5	DEALLOCATE	28
14.2D	When to use Cursors	29

Chapter 1 - Database Design

INTRODUCTION TO DATABASE DESIGN

Design theory

Querying a database does assume that the participant understands at least some database design theory. So the relational model is discussed and an introduction to the way data is organized, covering the degrees of data normalization and the Extended Relational Analysis (ERA) model.

Whole books have been written about this subject and the brief treatment here is merely a rehash of the main points. It is expected that anyone reading this chapter already has an understanding of these topics so it is really only included for completeness.

This book aims at stating things simply so that first-time users are not overwhelmed by detail. Concepts are actually fairly simple so a simplistic approach is followed. As a user gets to know SQL the concepts will be understood more and more until an in depth coverage is desired. In the beginning let's keep it as straight forward as possible.

Chapter 1: Database Design

Outline - The Context Tool

1	**Data, Design and Normalization**		**5**
1A	**Some definitions**		**5**
1B	**Database Design**		**6**
	1B.1	Hierarchical Design Model - One-to-Many	7
	1B.2	Network Design Model - Many-to-Many	9
	1B.3	Relational Design Model - Independent Data	9
	1B.4	Database Design Considerations	10
1C	**Normalization**		**11**
	1C.1	First Normal form	12
	1C.2	Second Normal form	13
	1C.3	Third Normal form	14
	1C.4	Benefits of Normalization	15
1D	**Denormalization**		**16**
	1D.1	Disadvantages of Normalization	16
1E	**Some suggestions for Normalized design**		**17**
1F	**Designing Tables**		**18**
1G	**Tradeoffs to Normalization**		**19**
2	**The ERA Model**		**20**
2A	**Entities**		**20**
2B	**Relationships**		**21**
	3B.1	Keys	22
2C	**Attributes**		**23**
2D	**Modeling Elements**		**24**
2E	**The Schema**		**24**

1 Data, Design and Normalization

1A   Some definitions

data
> In this context means the coded representation of information
>> for use in a computerized database system
>
> Data has attributes, such as type and length

database
> A collection of information, data tables, and other objects that are
>> organized and presented to serve a specific purpose,
>> such as facilitation of searching, sorting, and regeneration of data.
>
> Databases are stored in system files known as devices.

database management system (DBMS)
> A repository for the collection of computerized data files,
>> enabling users to perform a variety of operations on those files,
>> including retrieving, appending, editing, updating, and reporting

data definition
> The process of setting up databases and creating database objects,
>> such as tables, indexes, constraints, defaults, rules, procedures,
>> triggers, and views

database language
> The language used for accessing data in, querying, updating, and
>> managing relational database systems
>
> SQL is a widely used mathematical database language which uses set theory
>
> With SQL, you can retrieve data from a database, create databases and
>> database objects, add data, modify existing data, and perform
>> other complex functions
>
> You can also change the server configuration, modify database or
>> session settings, and control data and access statements
>
> Many of these capabilities are implemented by using one of
>> three SQL categories:

1. **data definition language (DDL)**
   A language for modeling the structure of a database (not the contents)
   It is used to create, modify, and remove databases and database objects

2. **data manipulation language (DML)**
   The subset of the SQL language used to retrieve and manipulate data

3. **data control language (DCL)**
   T-SQL statements that permit access to database objects

predicate

Scattered about the literature you will encounter the word predicate. In English this can be defined as "something about the subject or argument." We need to get a bit more specific and put this term into a database context. If you use the word 'FILTER' you will not far wrong and the filter describes the use of the code that makes up the predicate. So the predicate (filter) logic defines what you are trying to obtain. It defines the desired result set. Predicate calculus is that branch of symbolic logic that deals with propositions containing predicates, names and quantifiers. 'Predicate' was derived from the Latin word praedicare from prae (before) and dicare (make known)

object

An object is a thing – having said that we can say that it is like a noun (in the English language). It is described with adjectives (properties) and you can do stuff (technical term) by using verbs (an action, 'a doing word' or method)
An object belongs to a type of object (called a class)
At this point it is only important to know that a table is a database object and so is a view and also an index

1B Database Design

A database has both a physical design and a logical design

Design
Physically, SQL Server uses XML but we are not concerned here with the physical.
Here we are condidering the <u>logical</u> design which is created with a <u>business problem</u> in mind (not the software)

A **logical** design produces the database schema which defines:
1. what information is stored
2. how the data is organized
3. what tables are needed
4. what columns are needed in each table

Note:
1. Designs should work on paper
2. Business processes may change
3. Logical **design** is independent of the software

Implementation of the Logical Database Design
(also known as the **physical** implementation) involves:
1. determining storage space for the:
   - database
   - device
   - transaction log
2. creating the tables
3. selecting primary keys and foreign keys

In SQL Server the database schema is implemented by using DDL (Data Definition Language)

Data Integrity Requirements (Designing & Implementing)
The Implementor can assign **restrictions** to certain data, for example:
- implement **default** values
- implement **rules** that enforce data integrity

Programming the Database Server

includes:
- writing batches of commands
- triggers
- scripts
- stored procedures

that can:
- enforce data integrity
- provide information to users
- automate administrative functions
- manage server operations

can also include methods of communicating with:

1. clients, by using:
   - ODBC
   - DB-Library
   - SQL-DMO

2. other servers & platforms - by using remote stored procedures

3. outside the server - by using extended stored procedures

Data Modeling

Creating the database design starts with the **Data Model**

There are 3 basic designs to choose from:
1. Hierarchical
2. Network
3. Relational

and lately - 'object orientated' (but this is beyond our scope here)

1B.1   Hierarchical design model - one-to-many

Data is represented in an inverted tree structure,
> the top level being considered the root

Each level is dependent on the on the one above
Each level can have a one-to-many relationship with the one below

Data is arranged in a single file, further arranged into individual trees
of different types containing links connecting occurrences

The most important point is that no record can ever exist without its superior record

Example of Hierarchical Design

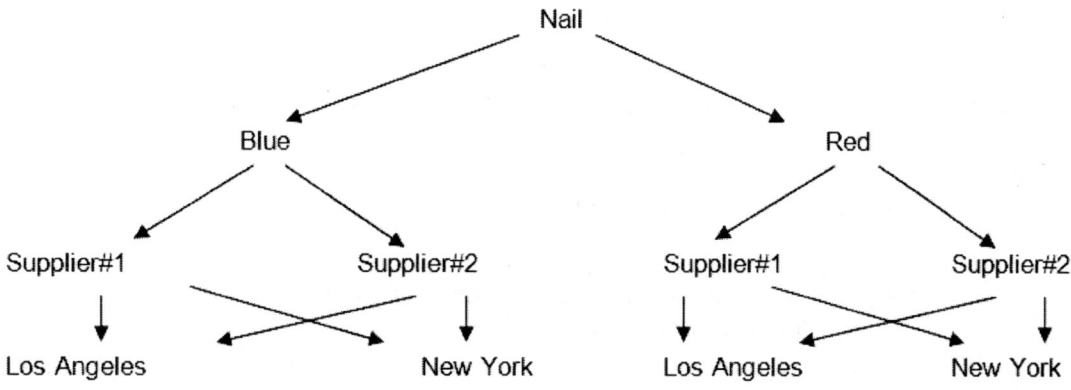

with **pointers** forming the links between e.g. Red and Suppliers 1 & 2
These pointers are actual links that exist and need to be maintained (updated) in the database

Systems that can be considered hierarchical include:
> IBM's IMS
> Informatics' MarkIV
> MRI's System 2000
> FoxPro (at least until DBC)
> dBase

Database Design

1B.2 Network design model - many-to-many

Data is represented by records and links in a more
> general structure than used in the hierarchical model

A record can have any number of superiors and any number of dependents

Thus this allows a many-to-many model
> It achieves this by using 'connector' records (links)

It achieves greater flexibility
> but applications are tightly coupled to the database

Examples are:

UNIVAC's	DMS 100
Cullinane's	IDMS
IBM's	DBOMP

1B.3 Relational design model - passive independent data

Hierarchical models and Network designs use pointers
> embedded in the physical records

A true relational system uses no such pointers,
> instead it uses **relational algebra** to **match** data values
>> - there are NO pointers

Each set of related information is stored in a table (hence the name relational). A RDBMS Relational Database Management System can be further explained as a management system for a bunch of tables. Each table containing a set of related information

It follows, therefore, that each table is passive and physically independent

Data is stored in a number of tables with a fixed number
> of columns and a variable number of rows
>> - Records are referred to as Rows
>> - Fields are referred to as Columns

Relational databases use algebraic set theory and predicate logic to compare items of data in the fields of rows to filter out the data that does not apply leaving the data that does

Associations between records are based on data values in fields
> (these values form a 'domain' for the field). Rows form instances of the items defined by the column list of the table. Rows used to me called 'tuples" so if you see that term just think of rows

Database Design

The columns are defined as headers while rows are defined as the values for an instance of the set of rows (table)

Relationships between tables are defined in terms of fields that contain a value - called Keys - Primary and Foreign that is the same in both tables. Unlike the hierarchical and network models the relational model matches values rather than 'links' between data

A Primary key is a column (or columns) that contains only a unique value. This can be matched with the values in a Foreign key of another table. The PK table is termed a Parent and the FK table termed the child table. If the FK is unique then you have a one-one relationship otherwise you have a one-many relationship

Using 'set' algebra, there are precise operations that can be carried out on the data, yielding defined and predictable results (see definition of predicate)

    e.g.   Where the value in column A = 123
             Where the value in column B > 100

Items that 'pass' the defined definition criteria will be subject to appropriate action

Values can be read from one table and used as the criteria to search other tables

The result of a query is known as the ResultSet

Benefits of the Relational model are:
- Simplicity
- Data independence
- A sound mathematical foundation
- Symmetry - equal ease of access, no matter what criteria is involved

Applications are **loosely** coupled to the database
The focus is on what data is needed rather than on how to get it

Note: Relational databases differ from non-relational databases in that there are no system dependencies stored within the data; by contrast, hierarchical databases are not relational because they contain pointers (links) to other data

Examples of Relational systems include:
    Microsoft SQL Server
    Ingress

Oracle
Informix
Sybase SQL Server
IBM's   DB2
MySQL

1B.4   Database Design Considerations

A well-designed database performs well

Designing a database requires an understanding of both:

1. the business functions you want to model
2. the database concepts and features used to represent those business functions.

Once implemented it usually extremely time consuming and difficult to change the design of a database significantly.

When designing a database, you should:
- Design a database plan to fit your purpose.
- Use Normalization rules where appropriate (which is most of the time) to prevent mistakes in design.
- Consider data integrity.
- Design the Security requirements of the database and user permissions.
- Design for the performance needs of the application.
- Ensure that the database design takes advantage of SQL Server features that improve performance.
- Aim to achieve a balance between the size of the database and the hardware configuration. This is important for performance.
- Design for ease of database maintenance.
- Estimate the likely size of the database.

1C Normalization

The process of organizing data in a database is called Normalizing

Having reviewed the benefits of Relational design
> it follows that we have to now consider the design of the tables in which we will store data

Goals of Database design:
- have a logical structure to the data
- minimize duplications where appropriate (reduce redundancy)
    - thus avoiding inconsistency of data
- eliminate update, insert and delete anomalies
- eliminate the risk of data loss enhance maintainability, extensibility and performance

There are rules of database design (called normalization rules),
> each table should describe one type of entity - a person, place, event, or thing.

While there are more degrees of Normalization
> the third normal form is generally sufficient to meet the goals

The First 6 (of 12) Rules of Normalization are:

1. Remove repeating or multivalued attributes
2. Remove attributes that are not dependent on the primary key
3. Remove transitory dependent attributes

A common way to remember this is that:
attributes should depend upon the key, the whole key and nothing but the key

Boyce/Codd Normal form: Ensure 3rd Normal form for all parts of Primary keys

4. Remove any independently multivalued components of the
    primary key to two new parent tables
5. Remove pairwise cyclic dependencies

Boyce/Codd, 4th and 5th are listed only for completeness and 6-12 are omitted completely

This includes creating tables and establishing relationships between those tables
> according to rules designed both to
>> - protect the data and
>> - to make the database more flexible
>
> by eliminating two factors:
>> - redundancy and
>> - inconsistent dependency

1C.1 First Normal Form

Rule: Data must have only 2 dimensions.
Atomic values are non-decomposable
i.e. there is:
never more than one set of values (domain) for
any one attribute (field, column)
This means only **one value** in any column

Method:
Eliminate groups of data in individual tables by creating extra rows
Do not use multiple fields in the same row to store similar data

Examples: Converting to First Normal Form

Exercise 1   Part Number and Supplier

Not in 1NF

Part	Suppliers		
Part#1	Supplier#1	Supplier#2	Supplier#3

In 1NF

Part	Supplier
Part#1	Supplier#1
Part#1	Supplier#2
Part#1	Supplier#3

Exercise 2   Name

Not in 1NF

Name

Cliff H Beacham

In 1NF

FirstName	Initial	LastName
Cliff	H	Beacham

1C.2 Second Normal Form

Rule: Eliminate redundant data
Every table is in 1NF plus
Every record in a table has a primary key and every
   non-key attribute is fully dependent on the primary key

Example:

1NF *Product Table*

PartID
PartDescription
PartCost
SupplierID
SupplierName
SuppAddress
SuppCity

2NF

Part Table		*Supplier Table*	
PartID	PK	***SupplierID**	PK
PartDescription		SuppName	
PartCost		SuppAddress	
PartSupplierID*	FK	SuppCity	
		SuppState	
		SuppZip	

Note well: Do not use the table name in column headings as above (see Tips chapter)

Notice: The Cost still depends on the Product but not the Supplier Name or Part Description
(If you think further about it you might conclude that this design
   characteristic is a management policy decision - whether to set a
   cost according to the part and use that as a standard cost or to
   enter a price from each supplier). The cost can be a calculated
   field also, depending on an average, the last cost or some other basis)

PK = Primary Key
FK = Foreign Key

So the trick is to break out the information that is causing redundancy of data
   and put it in another table with a Foreign Key on the child table
   matching the value of the Primary Key of the parent table

Note: Parent table are the table that contain the Foreign Keys are contained in the child tables. Primary Keys are the parent tables. So the Supplier table is the Parent and the Part table is the child to the Supplier parent.

You cannot have a child with no parent – you cannot have a Part with no supplier. However, you can have a Supplier with no Parts or a Parent (Potential parent) with no children

1C.3 Third Normal Form

Rules: Every field depends **only directly** on the Primary Key

1. Every table is in 2NF and
2. Every non-key attribute is non-transitively (directly)
   dependent on the primary key
   i.e. Every non-key is mutually independent

Example 1 - Using the 2NF from the previous example:

Part Table		*Supplier Table*
PartID*	PK	*SupplierID
PartDescrip		SuppName
PartCost		SuppAddress
SupplierID*	FK	SuppCity
		SuppState
		SuppZip*

3NF is therefore:

Part Table		*Supplier Table*		*ZipCodes Table*	
PartID*	PK	*SupplierID	PK	*Zip	PK
PartDescrip		SuppName		State	
PartCost		SuppAddress			
SupplierID*	FK	SuppCity			
		Zip*	FK		

This illustrates that although the State is dependent on the SupplierID it is **also** dependent on the Zip code and can be split out to another table to eliminate a redundancy. (However, see the next section for a discussion of why you might not do this in practice)

Note: Usually data is reduced to 3rd normal form and only denormalized when there is a very good reason

1C.4   Benefits of Normalization

The logical design of the database, including the tables and the relationships between them, is the core of an optimized relational database.

Good logical database design can lay the foundation for optimal database performance.

A poor logical database design can impair the performance of the entire system.

Normalizing a logical database design involves using formal methods to separate the data into multiple, related tables.

A greater number of narrow tables (with fewer columns) is characteristic of a normalized database.

A few wide tables (with more columns) is characteristic of an unnormalized database.

Reasonable normalization will often improve performance.

When useful indexes are available, the SQL Server query optimizer is efficient at selecting rapid, efficient joins between tables.

Some of the benefits of normalization include:
- Faster sorting and index creation.
- A larger number of clustered indexes.
- Narrower and more compact indexes.
- Fewer indexes per table, which improves the performance of INSERT, UPDATE, and DELETE statements.
- Fewer NULL values and less opportunity for inconsistency, which increase database compactness.

As normalization increases, so will the number and complexity of joins required to retrieve data.

Too many complex relational joins between too many tables can hinder performance.

Reasonable normalization often includes few regularly executed queries that use joins involving more than four tables.

Sometimes the logical database design is already fixed and total redesign is not feasible.

Even then, however, it might be possible to normalize a large table selectively into several smaller tables.

If the database is accessed through stored procedures, this schema change could take place without affecting applications.

1D Denormalization

Sometimes it is beneficial to denormalize in an effort to increase performance or functionality. This is why the Zip Code/State table is not usually used

The general feeling among developers is that the database should be designed as fully normalized before denormalizing is considered and only then with a full understanding of the data and the needs of the user

1D.1 Disadvantages of Normalization

1. Too many complex joins can slow performance

    (you should limit the number tables joined to 4)

    e.g. if you have to look up the state from the zip code, every time you query an address you add a join to the query

2. There is an overhead involved with indexes and tables

3. CPU time is needed to handle perform joins and maintain data and referential integrity

1E Some suggestions for normalized design

In relational database design theory, normalization rules identify certain attributes that must be present or absent in a well-designed database.

While a complete discussion of normalization rules goes well beyond the scope of this topic, there are a few rules that can help you achieve sound database design:

- **All tables should have a column to identify a row uniquely.**

    The fundamental rule of database design theory is that each table should have a unique row identifier, a column or set of columns that can be used to distinguish any single record from every other record in the table.

    Each table should have an ID column, and no two records can share the same ID value.

    The column or columns serving as the unique row identifier for a table are the primary key of the table.

- **Tables should store only data for a single type of entity.**

    Attempting to store too much information in a table can prevent efficient and reliable management of the table's data. In the preceding example of the **pubs** database, the titles and publishers information is stored in two separate tables.

    While it is possible to have columns for both the book and its publisher's information in the titles table, this design leads to several problems, including - the publisher information must be added and stored redundantly for each book

- **A table should not have repeating values or columns.**

    The table for an item in the database should not contain a list of values for a specific piece of information.

    For example, a book in the **pubs** database could be coauthored.

    If there is a column in the **titles** table for the name of the author, this presents a problem.

    One solution is to store the name of both authors in the column, but this makes it difficult to show a list of the individual authors.

    Another solution is to change the structure of the table to add another column for the name of the second author, but this accommodates only two authors.

    Yet another column must be added if a book has three authors.

If you find that you need to store a list of values in a single column, or if you have multiple columns for a single piece of data (**au_lname1**, **au_lname2**, and so on), you should consider placing the duplicated data in another table with a link back to the primary table.

The **pubs** database has a table for book information and another table that stores just the ID values for the books and the IDs of the books' authors.

This design allows any number of authors for a book without modifying the definition of the table and allocates no unused storage space for books with a single author.

1F Designing Tables

When you design a database, you decide what tables you need, what type of data goes in each table, who can access each table, and so on.

As you create and work with tables, you continue to make more detailed decisions about them.

The most efficient way to create a table is to define everything you need in the table at one time, including its data restrictions and additional components.

However, you can also create a basic table, add some data to it, and then work with it for a while.

This approach gives you a chance to see what types of transactions are most common and what types of data are frequently entered before you commit to a firm design by adding constraints, indexes, defaults, rules, and other objects.

It is a good idea to outline your plans on paper before creating a table and its objects.

Decisions that must be made include:

- Types of data the table will contain.
- Columns in the table and the data type (and length, if required) for each column.
- Which columns accept null values.
- Whether and where to use constraints or defaults and rules.
- Types of indexes needed, where they are needed, and which columns are primary keys and which foreign keys.

1G Tradeoffs to normalization.

A database that is used primarily for decision support (DSS) as opposed to update-intensive transaction processing (OLTP) may not have redundant updates and may be more understandable and efficient for queries if the design is not fully normalized.

Unnormalized data is a more common design problem than over-normalized data.

Starting with a normalized design and then selectively denormalizing tables for specific reasons is a good strategy.

Whatever the database design, you should take advantage of features in SQL Server to automatically maintain the integrity of your data and make the data rules visible to all users of the database, rather than hiding them in application logic.

- CHECK constraints ensure that column values are valid.
- DEFAULT and NOT NULL constraints avoid the complexities (and opportunities for hidden application bugs) caused by missing column values.
- PRIMARY KEY and UNIQUE constraints enforce the uniqueness of rows (and implicitly create an index to do so).
- FOREIGN KEY constraints ensure that rows in dependent tables always have a matching master record.
- IDENTITY columns efficiently generate unique row identifiers.
- TIMESTAMP columns ensure efficient concurrency checking between multiple-user updates.
- User-defined data types ensure consistency of column definitions across the database.

1H The ERA Model

The Extended **R**elational **A**nalysis model explains the data modeling concepts involved in producing a fully normalized database. It consider
>Entities
>Relationships
>Attributes

Note: ERA conveniently has the same initials as **E**ntities, **R**elationships and **A**ttributes

1H.1 Entities

An Entity is like a noun - it is an object

Entities are modeled in a database as a table of records

Records (Rows) within the table are **different from all other Rows** i.e. they are **unique**

It seems to be a source of confusion that Entity integrity is enforced by the uniqueness of rows. This may be because a row is an **instance** of an entity.

Tables (Entities)

>A database can contain many tables

Tables:
>- have unique names
>- are composed of Rows and Columns

Columns:
>- describe an attribute of the entity
>- can be in any order

Rows:
>- describe one occurrence (instance) of the entity
>- their order is not significant
>>(we can manipulate it however we wish)
>- a row applies only to one table
>>but is part of a 'complete record'
>>(not to be confused with 'record' which used to mean a row in a single table)

Table restrictions

>Table names must be unique within a database
>Column names must be unique within a table
>Rows must be unique within a table
>>- this is enforced by having a unique primary key

Database Design

1H.2 Relationships

Relationships are defined by keys

Keys can be Primary keys or Foreign keys
 which refer to fields (columns) in a table

They are stored in a column in a table or in their own table
 depending on the type of relationship

Type	Stored in
one-to-one	column – column
one-to-many	column – column
many-to-many	table containing 2 columns for the keys

1H.2a one-to-one (1:1)

This can be used to:
 - decrease the number of columns in a single table
 - increase the opportunity for indexing effectively
 - breakout certain columns for security reasons (eg Salaries)

Implemented by: Use the same PK for each table

1H.2b one-to-many (1:n)

The classic 1:n relationship is what enables normalization

To implement a **one-to-many** relationship - the relationship is stored using a special column in the n-side table which stores the primary key of the 1-side row.

Note: If the primary key comprises of more than one column you have to use the same number of columns.

1H.2c many-to-many (n:m)

Implemented with the help of a junction table which stores the primary keys of related rows. The combination is unique and builds the primary key of our junction table itself.

The junction table stores the primary keys of each table that is involved in the relationship to store each possible combination of primary keys which itself is unique again.

As an example of a many to many relationship look at the many-to-many relationships in the pubs database. The authortitle table defines a many-to-many relationship between authors and book titles. i.e. an author can write many books and a book can have more than one author. Notice the arrows in the schema are labeled N to N.
 (the pubs schema is at the back of the doc set)

1l Keys

1l.1 Primary Keys (PK)

Every table can (not must) have one
    and only one primary key
    which must have a unique index

Therefore the PK column must not permit:
- Nulls
- Duplicates
- Changes

This enforces data integrity

The Primary Key constraint enforces the 'NOT NULL' and 'No Duplicates' constraints

1l.2   Foreign Keys (FK)

A Foreign Key references the primary key of the same
    or another table

A column can be
- the Primary key of its own table
- the Foreign key of another table
- a Null

Advantages of creating a Foreign key

- SQL Server checks the values in the FK column against the values in the PK column to which it refers

- It provides a virtual link between two tables

1J Attributes

Attributes are like adjectives - they **describe** entities (nouns)
They are modeled as columns (data fields) in a table

ERA Model Component	Example	Old Name
Entity	Customers	Rows
Entity	Orders	Rows
Relationship	Orders - Customer	Link
Attribute	Name	Field name
Attribute	Address	Field name
Attribute	Phone Number	Field name
Attribute	Product ID	Field name

Another source of confusion is that the value in a field is an element not an attribute
(the column/field name is the attribute

Non-decomposable Columns (Attributes)

Non-decomposable Columns are columns that cannot be
further analyzed into smaller usable columns
e.g. John H Smith
Should be in three columns

The benefits of this are:
- easier to update
- easier to query (you will not have to parse)
- better data integrity (Types, Rules, Defaults & Constraints)

Column Restrictions

1 Not Null
is a restriction that requires an entry in a column

2 No Duplicates
requires every value in the column to be unique

3 No changes
a column value once entered cannot be changed
(primary keys are a good example)

1K Modeling Elements

Can be thought of as:
      Tables   with their restrictions
      Columns   with their restrictions
      Keys   both primary and foreign
With these elements, data is modeled in the schema

1L The Schema

A database schema describes the current structure of the tables in the database.

Another way of thinking of it is that it is the database without the data

In more detail it covers the definition of the total database layout, including:
- integrity checks and
- persistent relationships among tables and their indexes

Note: The pubs schema is at the back of the Transact-SQL Reference
also the schema for SQL Server itself

Further Reading:
Technet,

Planning Tables

After planning the schema it would seem appropriate to give some thought to the tables themselves

Decisions will be needed, including:

1. what type of data the table will contain
2. what columns you need in the table including datatypes (and length)
3. which columns should accept null values
4. whether to use constraints and/or defaults and rules and if so, where
5. what types of indexes and where
6. which columns should be the primary and foreign keys

Database Design

CHAPTER 2:

D A T A B A S E S   O B J E C T S

This includes tables

While this chapter may seem to be out of order, it has been included here so that it can serve as a reference. Perhaps the best way to cover this is to read this chapter lightly, not being concerned about an in-depth understanding and refer back to it when you need to later.

Books are written for several purposes. They can be courseware for teaching purposes, they can also be a reference or a dictionary. While you cannot learn English from a Dictionary you might not be able to learn English without one. So we will look at some training databases and then go on to discuss some of the components – this chapter will probably not add too much to overall understanding but we should cover the topics sooner or later so let's do it sooner.

> Quote from Alice in Wonderland (Lewis Carroll)
> "Rule Forty-two. All persons more than a mile high to leave the court."

So following Alice's instruction we will dispense with the complex (mile-high) and take a first look at the sample databases that come with earlier versions of SQL Server.

Then database components. including datatypes.

To use queries successfully you have to know that system stored procedures exist and can be used in your queries.

The CREATE TABLE statement is also briefly included.

Chapter 2 – Database Objects

DATABASE OBJECTS

Outline - The Context Tool

1	**Database components**	4
1A	User databases	4
	1A.1 The pubs database	4
	1A.2: The Northwind Database	4
1B	Database Components	5
	1B.1 Database Objects	5
	1B.2 Indexes	5
	1B.3 Datatypes	5
	1B.4 Constraints	5
1C	System Stored Procedures	6
2	**Creating Tables**	7
2A	Datatypes	7
	2A.1 System Supplied Datatypes	7
	2A.2 NULL	8
	2A.3 User-defined Datatypes	9
	2A.4 Special Datatypes	9
	2A.5 Exact and Approximate Data	10
	2A.6 Adding and Dropping Datatypes	10
2B	The Create Table Statement	11
	2B.1 Temporary Tables	12
	2B.2 Drop Table Statement	12
	2B.3 Alter Table Statement	13

2A Database Components

2A.1 User Databases

these are created by the user - e.g. Pubs

2A.1a The pubs sample database

Microsoft used to include the *pubs* training database with its product
It is contained in the master device
It is based on a schema covering the distribution of books
Included with the product is the script - which will generate
    11 tables and other objects and then populate them with data

Exercise:

In SQL Enterprise Manager 1xClk on the **+** next to your Server
    in the access tree. Repeat for databases then objects
    then Tables

While the tables are small many books on SQL Server use the pubs database for examples which used to be including in the doc-set (document set) which came with the SQL Server product. These days you can download the scripts from Microsoft Archives. Try http://archive.msdn.microsoft.com/northwind/release/projectreleases.aspx or you can just Google to get a link to a downlaod source.

You cannot do any damage to the pubs database because you can
    run the *instpubs.sql* script (found in the *\MSSQL\INSTALL*
    directory) to reinstall it at any time

Exercise:

Open isql/w and FILE\OPEN\Choose instpubs.sql
    - run it in Query Analyser or SSMS

Note: Do not think of 2xClk'ing it – it is not an executable file. However you can open it in Notepad and copy the scipt into SSMS to run it.

Chapter 2 - Objects (Tables etc)

2A.1b The Northwind sample database (the MS Access sample database)

Exercise:
Once you have installed the Northwind database, use the console tree and choose the Server\Datbases\Northwind\Diagrams

RtClk and choose New Database Diagram, then work your way through the wizard adding all the tables. When you have finished you will see a complete schema of the database.

Many exercises are now being based upon this database so you need to get familiar with it as well as the pubs database.

Note: The current sample database is Adventureworks which may well be far tpp complex for a beginner to deal with, so we will refer to the 'pubs' databse in our examples. None of these databases are sold and are freely available as training databases so there are no copyright issues.

2B   Database Components

2B.1   Database Objects

(type sp_help *also* SELECT * FROM sysobjects)

Objects contain objects
A **database** object contains other objects, such as:
- *tables*
- *views*
- *stored procedures*
    which interact with data

You should query the sysobjects table to obtain a list of objects
    in a database

Object	Description
Table	Collection of Columns and Rows
View	An alternate way of looking at data from >= 1 table It is a stored query result set (sometimes called a virtual table)
Default	Column value if none entered
Rule Stored Procedure	Precompiled collection of SQL statements
Trigger	Automatically executed special form of stored procedure

2B.2   Indexes (type sp_helpindex *tablename*)

An index is a set of ordered table rows
>   which point to the unordered rows in a data table

See the chapter on Indexes – yes, there really is a whole chapter.

Query sysindexes to obtain a list of indexes in the database

2B.3   Datatypes (type SELECT * FROM systypes)

A type specifies the type of information in a column and how it is stored

For example: Char(12) is a character with a fixed length of 12 characters

Query the systypes table to obtain a list of datatypes in the database

2B.4   Constraints (type sp_help constraints)

Constraints place a restriction on the values that may be entered
>   in a column or table

Query the sysconstraints and sysreferences tables to obtain a list of constraints

Note:
>   sp_help *tablename* will display index, constraint and default information

2C System Stored Procedures

A system procedure is a precompiled collection of SQL statements
They are an easy way to query the system tables for administration and management activities
They are located in the *master* database
Some of them are:

System Procedure	*returns:*
sp_helpuser	list of users
sp_columns *tablename*	details of columns, views, parameters
sp_helptext *objectname*	SQL definition statements
sp_depends	references
sp_helpindex *tablename*	indexes
sp_helpkey	keys
sp_help	database objects
sp_stored_procedures	views, rules, defaults, triggers and stored procedures
sp_protect	user permissions
sp_helpsegments	segments
sp_help *typename*	datatype
sp_helpconstraint	reference constraints
sp_help *tablename*	reference constraints (ditto above
sp_helparticle	articles for replication
sp_helppublication	publications
sp_helpsubscriberinfo	subscriber info
sp_helpsort	displays character set & sort order
sp_configure	configurable environmental variables
sp_helpdb	databases on SQL Server
sp_helpdevice	available disk devices and databases
sp_helplanguage	languages registered
sp_lock	active locks
sp_addmessage	add a system error messages
sp_drop message	drop a system error messages
sp_processinfo	ongoing processes
sp_remotelogin	remote user accounts
sp_helpserver	remote servers
sp_spaceused	disk space allocated to each database
sp_dropdevice	drops a device
sp_disk default	to set a default
sp_dboption	lists and sets database options

These descriptions are obviously too brief and further research will be necessary before use

Note: there is no particular order or grouping of the above, each has its use and importance depending on circumstances

2D   Creating Tables

Before creating tables it may be wise to look at the datatypes that
    will be used to store data in the table columns

Datatypes have to exist before you can refer to them in a CREATE TABLE
    statement that defines a default using that datatype

2D.1   Datatypes

Datatypes are pre_defined, named methods for categories of data
You cannot create a completely new class of data; you can only
    define subclasses in the existing datatypes

Datatype selection is very important because:
        space utilization
        performance implications
        reliability
        manageability
        you cannot change a tables datatypes
            (you have to drop the table and recreate it)

2D.2 System supplied Datatypes

Datatypes define what type of data a column can hold

	Type of Data	Datatype	Storage size
1	Binary	binary(n) varbinary(n)	255 fixed 255 variable
2	Character char	 varchar	255 fixed 255 variable
3	Date & Time	datetime smalldatetime	8 bytes 4 bytes
4	Exact numeric	decimal numeric	2-17 bytes depending on precision 2-17 bytes depending on precision
5	Approx numeric	float real	8 bytes 4 bytes
6	Integer	int smallin tinyint	4 bytes 2 bytes 1 byte
7	Monetary	money smallmoney	8 bytes 4 bytes
8	Special	bit timestamp user defined dataypes text & image text image	1 byte variable 2GB variable 2GB variable 2GB variable

2D.3 NULL

Although NULL is not a datatype it is definitely worthy of mention here
If a NULL is allowed, the column is designated variable length, even for a fixed length field
NULL means no entry has been made
>and usually implies that the value is either unknown or undefined

NULL allows you to distinguish between:
1 a 0 or a blank
>and
2 an unknown or inapplicable entry (both numeric and character columns)

NOT NULL is the default for SQL Server

NOT NULL - can also be used in a WHERE clause
>to retrieve all values except those that are NULL

If the user fails to make an entry in a column that allows null values,
>SQL Server supplies the value NULL (unless a default exists)

Defining columns as NULL provides a place holder for unknown data

Example: in the *titles* table, *price*, is set up to allow NULL
However, *title_id* and *title* do not allow null values
>since a NULL columns would make the row meaningless

When you create a table, define columns as NOT NULL when
>the information in the column is critical
>to the meaning of the other columns

When inserting data, the DEFAULT keyword can be used to insert NULL into a column

DEFAULT constraints defined on the table or user-defined defaults
>can be connected with either NULL or NOT NULL columns

An expression with a comparison operator evaluates to false
>if any of the operands is NULL
This means that null values never match another value
>(not even another NULL) when used with a comparison operator

Use NULL or IS NOT NULL to find null values in queries
>(when the columns being searched are defined as allowing nulls)

do not use = NULL
Use the ISNULL system function to replace null values in an expression with another value

Example: List all titles, their price (with zero instead of NULLs), their type and quantity sold
SELECT title, ISNULL(price, 0), type, ISNULL(ytd_sales, 0) from titles

If you try to find null values in columns defined as NOT NULL, SQL Server generates an error message

Null values are never joined or referenced, not even to other null values (e.g. in the case of a FOREIGN KEY constraint),

The empty string is never evaluated as NULL
- (' ') or (" ") is always stored as a single space in variables
- column data. 'abc' ' ' 'def' is equivalent to 'abc def', but not to 'abcdef'

2D.4   User defined Datatypes

User defined Datatypes are defined by the user for a specific database

They are : *defined in terms of the datatypes listed above*
- *included in the model database*
- *automatically included in all subsequent databases created*
- *added as a row in the systypes table*

Examples of how user-defined datatypes are based upon system datatypes:

Defined Datatype:	**Would map to system type:**
binary VARYING	varbinary
char VARYING	varchar
character(n)	char(n)
character	char(1)
character VARYING	varchar(n)
dec	decimal
double precision	float
float(n) for 1 - 7	real
float(n) for 8 - 15	float
integer	int

Example: Social Security Number 999-99-9999 is 11 characters
Note: We have to enclosed the datatype name in single quotes because it contains punctuation

sp_addtype ssn, 'varchar(11)', NOT NULL

Example: Telephone number (714) 555-1212

sp_addtype ssn, 'varchar(14)', NULL

2D.5 Special Dataypes

bit:
- Is a datatype that holds either 1 or 0
- Other Integer values (not 1 or 0) are always interpreted as 1
- Storage size is 1 byte
- Multiple *bit* types in a table can be collected into bytes
  - e.g.   7-bit columns fit into 1 byte
  - 9-bit columns take 2 bytes
- The *status* column in the *syscolumns* system table indicates
  - the unique offset position for *bit* columns
- Columns of type *bit* cannot be NULL or have indexes
- Use *bit* for true/false or yes/no types of data

timestamp:
- Is a datatype that is automatically updated every time a row
  - containing a *timestamp* column is inserted or updated
- Values in *timestamp* columns are *binary*(8) *varbinary*(8) data,
  - indicating the sequence of SQL Server activity on the row
- A table can have only one *timestamp* column
- The *timestamp* datatype has no relation to the system time
  - - it is simply a monotonically increasing counter
  - whose values will always be unique within a database
- If you do not supply a datatype, a column named *timestamp* is
  - automatically defined as a *timestamp* datatype
- You can name a column *timestamp* and assign it another datatype
- By default, the *timestamp* datatype is defined as *binary*(8)
- If used with NOT NULL, *timestamp* will be stored as *varbinary*(8)
- In client applications, the metadata declares the *timestamp* as
  - *varbinary*, regardless of the nullability
- The current *timestamp* value for a database can be selected with the
  - global variable @@DBTS

2D.6 Exact and Approximate Numeric Data

Exact: consists of data with accuracy to the least significant digit
Approximate: includes real and float types

There are 2 types, decimal and numeric
      Numeric is always exact while
      Decimal may provide greater precision than that specified

Both types are able to specify the degree of precision and scale

    Precision: Maximum total number of digits that can be stored
                          (includes both sides of the decimal point)

    Scale: Maximum number of digits that can be stored
                           to the right of the decimal point

Characteristics of Datatypes

Type	Precision	Default	Scale	Scale Default
decimal (p,s)	1-38	18	1-p	0
numeric (p,s)	1-38	18	1-p	0
float(n)	1-15			
real	1-7			
float	8-15			
double precision	8-15	15		

Note: At startup the precision level can be specified (max = 28)

Double precision is an 8 byte floating point number which is as
      accurate as the binary numbering system allows

2D.7 Adding and Dropping Datatypes

Adding

Syntax:

EXEC sp_addtype typename, phystype, nulltype

phystype is the name of the system defined datatype from which the user defined subtype is being created

a length has to be specified for char, varchar, binary & varbinary

nulltype is optional
it is disregarded if a NULL or NOT NULL is specified in th CREATE TABLE statement

Examples:

EXEC sp_addtype zipcode, 'char(10)'
EXEC sp_addtype longstring, 'varchar(75)'

Dropping

Syntax:

sp_droptype typename
cannot be dropped if tables reference it (or other database objects)

Example:

EXEC sp_droptype zipcode

2E The CREATE TABLE statement

Basic Syntax: CREATE TABLE databasename.owner.tablename
           (column_name, column_properties constraints.....)

Note: Constraints will be covered later

If you do not specify a segment name SQL Server uses a default

Maximum sizes
Number of Tables   Used to be 2 billion now only limited by space available
Columns per Table   Used to be 250 columns per table now 4096

So from a practical point of view – do not worry about limitations – they are so high you will not encounter them

Column names must be unique within each table

A datatype must be named for each column

In the column definition you can use the IDENTITY property to
       generate incremental values for the rows
           based on *seed* and *increment*
You can have a maximum of 1 identity column per table
Note: The identity type will limit the number of rows in the table
       e.g int (integer type) will limit the table to 32K rows

Note: the ID column is a special **attribute** - do not look at it as data, although it can act like data it is not completely the same as data

Example:

```
CREATE TABLE  member
(
member_no     numeric ( 6, 0 ) identity ( 1, 1 ),
lastname      varchar ( 30 )              NOT NULL,
firstname     varchar ( 30 ) ,
middleinitial char ( 1 )                  NULL,
photo         image                       NULL
)
```

Question 1:   How many rows will be the maximum for the above created table?
Question 2:   Does firstname have a NULL or NOT NULL option set?
Hint: see section 2D.3

2E.1 Temporary Tables

SQL Server supports two types of temporary tables: local and global.

> A local temporary table is:
> - visible only to the connection that created it
> - named with a # sign
>
> A global temporary table is:
> - available to all connections
> - named with a double ## sign

Note In addition to naming a temporary table with # or ##, temporary tables can be created without the pound sign by qualifying the table name with *tempdb* as the database

> e.g. **CREATE TABLE tempdb . . #[#]***table_name*
> (*column_definition*
> [, *next_column_definition*]...)

If created in *tempdb*, the table will exist until SQL Server is shutdown

2E.2 The DROP TABLE statement

Syntax: **DROP TABLE databasename.owner.tablename**

> DropTable cannot be used to drop a table that is being referenced by the Foreign key constraint
>
> Only the owner (or the administrator with reference to the owner) has permission (who has to specified in the DROP TABLE statement)
>
> Dropping a table results in removal of all data, indexes, triggers, constraints and permissions for that table
>
> Even if a table is empty it is not 'gone' until you drop it

2E.3 The ALTER TABLE statement

Syntax: **ALTER TABLE**   **databasename.owner.tablename**
[WITH NOCHECK]
[ADD
(CONSTRAINT | COLUMN_NAME | DEFAULT)

(options - depending on what type of alteration)
| DROP CONSTRAINT constraint_name]

Example:
The *authors* table has a column named *zip* that requires a 5-digit character string. The example adds a CHECK constraint to guarantee that only numbers are entered

ALTER TABLE authors
ADD
CONSTRAINT check_zip_format
CHECK (`zip LIKE '[0-9][0-9][0-9][0-9][0-9]'`**)**

The NOCHECK option is used to instruct SQL Server to either check existing values and Foreign key constraints or not

Note The WITH NOCHECK option will bypass checking FOREIGN KEY and CHECK constraints only at the time the table is altered.
Future data modifications made against any column will demand that all columns satisfy all CHECK constraints, even those columns not included in the UPDATE column list.

Do not confuse the NOCHECK option with the CHECK constraint

Drop the constraint by using:
ALTER TABLE authors
DROP CONSTRAINT check_zip_format

Primary key and Unique constraints are always checked

(See section on Constraints under Data Integrity)

Chapter 3 - SELECT

RETRIEVING DATA

This module is designed to enable you to:

Section 1 Write queries (SELECT statements) to retrieve specific columns

Section 2 Examine the various tools that can be employed in the process of SELECTing and manipulating data, including Expressions, Operators, Functions, Conversions and Search Arguements (SARGs)

Section 3 Write SELECT statements to retrieve specific rows, filtering by specific criteria

Section 4 Format and sort query results

SQL
The acronym SEQUEL was originally derived from "Structured English Query Language."

SQL was first used by Relational Software Inc (which is now called ORACLE)

SQL was made popular by IBM in DB2 about 1983

ANSI SQL-86 was established, and then ANSI SQL-89, but both were incomplete and did not provide an adequate standard for developer vendors to follow.

The ANSI-92 standard, however, jumped ahead and has defined a language which is almost a wish list. Even Microsoft has not been able to implement all the features.
e.g. - a datatype called interval and
- being able to use mixed character sets within the same table

In addition, there are differences in definitions, e.g. the term database has a different meaning. Features that are missing from T-SQL include the ability to drop columns from tables and to alter column widths.

The news is not all bad, however, since SQL Server includes many great features that are not included in the standard, for example, the use of triggers, stored procedures and data replication.

In the previous chapters we have already used T-SQL to create databases and database objects, now we will move over to querying the data.

Note: T-SQL can be categorized into 3 types of syntax:

- DML - Data Manipulation Language
- which works on the contents (the data itself)
- DDL - Data Definition Language
- for structuring the database rather than the contents
- DCL - Data Control Language
- which controls program logic (see Control of Flow section)

Chapter 3:
Select

Outline - The Context Tool

3 The Construction of the SELECT Statement 5

3A	SELECT (specifying columns)	7
3B	INTO (output into a table)	13
3C	FROM (specifying tables)	14
3D	WHERE (specifying rows)	15
3E	GROUP BY (subtotals)	16
3F	HAVING (specifying rows for groups)	17
3G	ORDER BY (sorting)	18
3H	COMPUTE (summary information)	19

3 The Select Statement

While the select clause is the only required clause in a select statement, there are three clauses that are usually included:
> SELECT
> FROM
> WHERE

The FROM clause is necessary only in select statements that retrieve data from tables (which is almost always).

The WHERE clause is optional (as are all other clauses).

The full syntax of the select statement includes these phrases and keywords:

SELECT   [all | distinct] select_list
[INTO   [[database.]owner.]table_name]
[FROM   [[database.]owner.]{view_name|table_name
[WHERE   search_conditions]
[GROUP BY   [all] aggregate_free_expression [, aggregate_free_expression]...]
[WITH [ROLLUP | CUBE]]
[HAVING   search_conditions]
[ORDER BY
         {[[[database.]owner.]{table_name.|view_name.}]
         column_name | select_list_number | expression} [asc | desc]
         [,{[[[database.]owner.]{table_name|view_name.}]
         column_name | select_list_number | expression} [asc | desc]]...]
[COMPUTE   row_aggregate(column_name)[,
         row_aggregate(column_name)]...
   [BY   column_name [, column_name]...]]

Primary SELECT statement

The three keywords that make up the primary SELECT statement are:

SELECT	select_list
FROM	table_list
WHERE	search_conditions

Example:

SELECT	au_fname, au_lname
FROM	authors
WHERE	city = "Oakland"

We will look at each of the components in turn and in the order that they appear in the
complete syntax (see 1A to 1H following).
Then we will look closer at Search conditions and Expressions.

This chapter contains items that depend upon each other and which form, the proverbial chicken & egg loop scenario.
Work through the examples and read each section of text.
The whole should solidify by the time you finish the chapter.
It may take a couple of revisions, but this **is** the foundation of the language.

How Ambiguity between names is dealt with:

Object names (which includes table_names) do not need to be unique in a database.

However, column names and index names must be unique within a table or a view, and other object names must be unique for each owner within a database.

Database names must be unique on SQL Server.

You can uniquely identify a table or column by fully qualifying it with:

    the database name,
    the owner's name,
    and (for a column) the table or view name.

Each of these qualifiers is separated from the next by a period:

e.g. *[[database.]owner.]table_name*
[[database.]owner.]view_name

The database and owner names are optional.

The default value for *owner* is the current user

The default value for *database* is the current database.

Intermediate elements in a name can be omitted
and their positions indicated by periods,
as long as SQL Server has enough information to identify the object:
syntax: *database..table_name*
database..view_name

In the case of remote stored procedures, a procedure is qualified as follows:
syntax: *server.database.owner.procedure*
e.g.   *remotesvr.pubs.dbo.sp_who*

3A   SELECT
Simplified syntax: SELECT select_list

select_list contains expressions that will be returned in the result set.
They can be comprised of:

literals	- enclosed in quotes
column names	- field names
formulas	- any valid formula
subqueries	- see chapter 6

see list below

The SELECT * is the most basic statement in T SQL
    The * selects all the **columns** in the same order as they are stored

The syntax used for the complete command is:

SELECT [ALL|DISTINCT] select_list

ALL   retrieves all the **rows** in the result set
                (usually ALL is not specified since it is the default)

DISTINCT   includes only unique rows

    Note: NULLS are considered to be duplicates so only
           one NULL would be selected

The **select_list** - specifies the columns to be selected

Examples:
    SELECT count(DISTINCT au_lname) FROM authors
    SELECT count(au_lname) FROM authors
    SELECT count(*) FROM authors

Note: If there is an ambiguity in a table name, a qualifier (Table Owner
       and/or Table name or View name) should be used to clarify
       it is never wrong to include qualifiers but in this chapter we will not
       usually use them since we will deal with only 1 table at a time)

Examples to type into the pubs database for practice.

Note: some of the following will draw upon knowledge not yet covered.
Just type the code (in bold below) and run it - you will see what is meant as we progress

The **select_list** - specifies the columns to be selected and can be expressed in the form of the next 10 examples:

3A.1 *

The asterix means all columns – returned in the order they are stored in the table.

  e.g. SELECT *
      FROM   publishers

Note: This is slow and inefficient - it always better to select the columns even if we do want them all

Tip: In the 'good old days' when hardware was slower this made a difference to the speed of execution because the Database Engine had to work out the names of the columns. Currently this may not seem necessary due to the power we now have but it is still good practice to specify the columns even if they are the complete set of columns. However, it depends on what you are trying to do. SELECT * is still the preferred shortcut method when wanting to see what columns are in the table or just returning the complete set of columns. It is considered bad practice in a production situation

3A.2 a list of column names

in the order you want to see them, separated by commas

If you had: SELECT pub_ID, pub_name, city, state

You might want to separate the list into rows (this adds to its readability)

  e.g. SELECT pub_ID,
           pub_name,
           city,
           state
      FROM   publishers

Alternative:
  e.g. SELECT pub_ID
           , pub_name
           , city
           , state
      FROM   publishers

this allows you to exclude a column by using a - - comment indicator before the row – like this:

e.g.	SELECT	pub_ID,
		pub_name,
	--	city,
		state
	FROM	publishers

this adds to its readability

3A.3 column names and column headings

(with which you want to replace the column name)

There are 2 ways to do this:
- either   1   column_heading = column_name
- or   2   column_name column_heading

e.g.   **SELECT**
         PublisherID = pub_ID,
         Publisher = pub_name,
         city,
         state
   FROM   publishers

alternately any of the following will work:
e.g.   **"Publisher Id" = pub_id**
           pub_name   Publisher
           pub_name   "Publishers Name"

Square Brackets in Names

In addition you need to know that T-SQL any names that contain Keywords or Spaces in the name must be eclosed in [ ] (square brackets). While using square brackets may be essential to make your code work, it does detract from the readability of your code

Therefore, avoid them if you can but use them where necessary

When designing a table use descriptive names that do not contain keywords (e.g. table) and spaces are always considered a no-no

Note: column headings must be enclosed in quotes if spaces are used

3A.4 an expression

this can be: column name
constant
function
combination of the above connected by:
    operators (arithmetic, bitwise, comparison, string)
or a Subquery

Syntax: {constant | column_name | function | (Subquery)}
[{operator | AND | OR | NOT}]
{constant | column_name | function | (Subquery)} . . . .

Examples:

```
SELECT
    title,
    price,
    "Selling Price" = (price * 1.5)
FROM titles

SELECT
    Sales = ytd_sales * price,
    'To Author' =   (ytd_sales * price * royalty)/100,
    'To Publisher' = ytd_sales * price - (ytd_sales * price * royalty)/100
FROM titles
```

(see section 2 of this chapter for further discussion)

3A.5 the IDENTITYCOL keyword
(instead of the name of the column)

Because the pubs database does not have an example
we have to create a table of our own

Note: *Type the whole of the following code into isql/w and highlight only the section of code you wish to run, then press Ctrl-E or ALT-X*

(SQL Server will run only the highlighted code).
This is the best way to experiment when developing.

```
CREATE TABLE jobs1
    (job_id      smallint      IDENTITY(100,1),
     job_desc    varchar(30)   NOT NULL
          DEFAULT 'New title not yet finalized')
GO

INSERT Jobs1
VALUES(DEFAULT)
GO

SELECT * FROM Jobs1
GO
```

Note: *Now run the INSERT statement again and once again then run the SELECT statement. Notice the IDENTITY column values*

```
DROP TABLE Jobs1
GO
```

3A.6 global variables

e.g. @@rowcount (Note the double @ characters)

We'll get to the use of variables in code later - for now you might want to run the following global variables and see what SQL Server returns.

SELECT @@connections Number of logins

SELECT @@cpu_busy Amount of time ticks SQL Server has been working since SS last started

SELECT @@IDLE Amount of time ticks SQL Server has been idle since SS last started

SELECT @@max_connections Max number of connections which can be made to SS in the current environment. (Not the current setting)

SELECT @@version SQL Server version running

SELECT @@servername Name of the local Server

SELECT @@spid Current server process ID - spid column of the sysprocesses table

SELECT @@textsize Current setting of text or image option

3A.7 a local variable assignment

@variable = expression

Until you assign a value to a local variable its value is NULL

In the following example note the assignment of
@author_name = au_fname + au_lname

```
DECLARE    @author_name varchar(50)
SELECT     @author_name = au_fname + au_lname
FROM       authors
WHERE      au_lname = "Smith"
PRINT      @author_name
```

Note: the query will only return the first instance of the match
there is no loop

3A.8 a literal enclosed in quotes

e.g.
```
SELECT    au_fname, "ID Number", au_id
FROM      authors
WHERE     au_lname = "Smith"
```

3A.9 a nested subquery_

e.g.
```
SELECT    title
FROM      titles
WHERE     pub_id =
          (SELECT  pub_id
           FROM    publishers
           WHERE   pub_name = "New Moon Books")
```

3A.10 What not to do - Cartesian Product

As an experiment enter the following queries
(use CTRL-END to go to the bottom of the result set):

**10.1 SELECT * FROM titles		Note: you get 18 rows back**
**10.2 SELECT * FROM authors	Note: you get 23 rows back**
10.3 SELECT * FROM authors, titles
Note: you get 414 rows back which is the cartesian product of the authors table and the titles table (18 x 23 = 414 rows).

3B INTO

Simplified syntax: SELECT   select_list
                          INTO   new_table_name

Creates a new table based on the columns in the select list
and the rows chosen in the WHERE clause

The new table name must follow the same rules as in CREATE TABLE

The SELECT INTO is a 2 step operation

    1   it creates the table
    2   then inserts the data

If step 2 fails the new table will still be created but with no data

Example: 1.   SELECT   *
(Run these   INTO   #lowpricebooks
3 in turn)   FROM   titles
                           WHERE   price <10

                  2.   SELECT   *
                          FROM   #lowpricebooks

                  3.   DROP TABLE #lowpricebooks

To save as a permanent table the 'select into/bulkcopy' option should be set to ON (default is OFF)
You can set thi soption programmatically by this code:

        use pubs
        sp_dboption database_name, 'select into/bulkcopy', true

Note: because SELECT is a keyword <u>select into/bulkcopy</u> must be in single quotes

Also run the following:
                sp_dboption
    and   **sp_helpdb pubs**

3C FROM

Specifies all the specific tables used in the SELECT statement

FROM 'table' or 'view' is required whenever a column name is included in a query

If the reference is to another database the full path to the table must be spelled out using

Database.Owner.table_name|view_name

Each table name or view name can be given an **alias** either
1   for convenience and simplification of subsequent referencing
2   or to distinguish the roles a table|view plays in a query

Syntax:

    FROM   table_name1 alias1,   table_name2 alias2, ...

Examples:
1   **FROM**   **titles t, authors a, titleauthor ta**

2   **SELECT**   **a.au_fname, a.au_lname**
     FROM   **authors a**

Note: Example 2 uses a simplistic situation involving one table only. We are not ready for multiple tables yet so just accept that there is a useful purpose for aliases which we will look at later

When an alias has been specified it must **always** be used from then on

The Order of the tables in the FROM clause is not significant unless it is referred to by OUTER JOIN syntax

3D WHERE

Syntax:

   WHERE search_conditions

Specifies the search conditions for the resultset to be returned

There is no theoretical limit on the number of search conditions that can be included

The WHERE clause can be used in:
   SELECT
   INSERT
   UPDATE
   DELETE
   or following HAVING

See Chapter 4B - Choosing Rows for a more complete discussion

3E   GROUP BY

Specifies the groups into which the resultset will be divided

GROUP BY is an aggregating function itself and therefore
> it must be free from aggregates in its own conditions
> (an aggregate is an function such as sum, avg, etc)

Syntax:
> **GROUP BY [All] expression, expression, etc**
>
> *Note:*   **- expression must be aggregate_free**

Example:
> **SELECT type, pub_id, sales = sum(ytd_sales * price)**
> **FROM titles**
> **GROUP BY type, pub_id**

An aggregate may be specified in the select_list, in which case a summary value for each group will be included in the result set

These summary values can be referred to in a HAVING clause

Text and image datatypes cannot be used

Each item in the select_list must produce a single value for each group

You can group by a valid expression instead of a column_name even if it does not appear in the select_list

Null values in the GROUP BY column are placed in a single group

Aggregate functions in the select_list are:
> applied to each of the GROUPS or
> to the whole table (if there is no GROUP BY statement)

3E.1 Cube and Rollup (These are super aggregates)

Example:
Use the previous GROUP BY query - add rollup

```
SELECT  type, pub_id, sales = sum(ytd_sales * price)
FROM  titles
GROUP BY type, pub_id
WITH rollup
```

Note that the resultset includes the totals for each primary group - **type**

Now substitute Cube

```
SELECT  type, pub_id, sales = sum(ytd_sales * price)
FROM  titles
GROUP BY type, pub_id
WITH cube
```

Note that the resultset includes the totals for
  each primary group - **type**
  and each secondary group - **pub_id** (at the end of the report)

This resultset means:

pub_id / Type	0877	0736	1389	Total
business	0	56k	210k	**266k**
mod_cook	107k	0	0	**107k**
popular_comp	0	0	283k	**283k**
psychology	8k	131k	0	**139k**
trad_cook	249k	0	0	**249k**
Total	**365k**	**187k**	**493k**	**1045k**

3F HAVING

The HAVING clause relates to the GROUP BY statement in much the same way as the WHERE clause relates to the SELECT statement

The WHERE clause restricts the rows which are included in each group

The HAVING clause restricts which groups are included in the resultset they restrict the rows returned but not the calculations of aggregates

Syntax:
HAVING search_conditions

Example:

```
SELECT      type, sales = sum(ytd_sales * price)
FROM        titles
GROUP BY    type
HAVING      sum(ytd_sales * price) > 150000
```

3G ORDER BY

Sorts the rows by columns (up to 16 columns)

Can include items which do not appear in the select_list

NULL is sorted first in the sort order

The default sort order is asc (ascending)

Syntax:
    ORDER BY column_name list-Number expression ASC | DESC

Examples:

    SELECT   *
    FROM   authors
    ORDER BY   au_fname

    SELECT *
    FROM   authors
    ORDER BY   au_lname

You can sort by:
- column_name
- column heading (or alias
- an expression
- a number representing the position in the select_list (but the column must be in the select_list)

To find the sort-order that is current use *sp_helpsort* to display the 256 characters in the ASCII set

The default is case-insensitive ascending in dictionary order

Text and image columns cannot be used

Subqueries and view definitions cannot include a ORDER BY clause

Examples:

  1   SELECT   pub_id, type, price, title
        FROM   titles
        ORDER BY   2 Desc, 1

Note: type is descending and pub_id is Ascending (by default)

  2   SELECT   pub_id, type, price, title

Note: type is in ascending (by default) and price is not ordered within each type (default only applies to the first column)

3	SELECT	pub_id, type, price, title
	FROM	titles
	ORDER BY	2, 3 DESC

this can also be written as:

3a	SELECT	pub_id, type, price, title
	FROM	titles
	ORDER BY	type, price DESC

3H   COMPUTE

Used with row aggregate functions to generate summary values
Includes:
- SUM
- AVG
- MIN
- MAX
- COUNT

They appear as additional rows in the query results

COMPUTE can be used by itself to produce Grand Totals
COMPUTE BY will produce Sub-totals for each change in the ORDER BY
    (therefore you have to have an ORDER BY to use COMPUTE BY)

Syntax:
    COMPUTE row_aggregate(column_name),
        row_aggregate(column_name), row_aggregate(column_name), etc
    BY   column_name, column_name, column_name, etc

BY indicates that values for row aggregate functions are to be
    calculated for subgroups

Listing >1 item after BY breaks a group into subgroups
    and applies a function at each level

Examples:
```
SELECT type, price, Sales = (price * ytd_sales)
FROM titles
WHERE type LIKE '%cook'
COMPUTE sum(price * ytd_sales)
```

contrast the results with this example of COMPUTE BY

```
SELECT type, price, Sales = (price * ytd_sales)
FROM titles
WHERE type LIKE '%cook'
ORDER BY type, price
COMPUTE sum(price * ytd_sales) BY type
```

Note: If you use COMPUTE BY you have to use ORDER BY and the columns in the COMPUTE BY must be a subset of the columns in the ORDER BY clause

It cannot <u>skip</u> any expression

Example:
    For ORDER BY a, b, c
        COMPUTE BY can be any or all of:

            COMPUTE BY a, b, c
            COMPUTE BY a, b
            COMPUTE BY a

Chapter 4 - SELECT plus

CHAPTER 4:

SELECT - PLUS

This module takes the basic SELECT statement further, introducing

Chapter 4:
Select Plus

Outline - The Context Tool

4A   Expressions, Operators, Functions 20
4A.1   Expressions 20
4A.2   Operators 22
    4A.2a Arithmetic and Logical operators 22
    4A.2b Bitwise operators 23
    4A.2c Comparison operators 24
    4A.2d Join operators 25
    4A.2e String operators 26
    4A.2f Operators precedence 26
4A.3   Functions 27
    4A.3a Numeric functions 27
        4A.3a.1 Mathematical 27
        4A.3a.2 Aggregate 28
    4A.3b String (Character) functions 30
    4A.3c Datetime functions 31
    4A.3d System functions 32
        4A.3d.1 System tables 32
        4A.3d.2 Niladic functions 33
    4A.3e Converting datatypes 34
    4A.3f Text and Image functions 34

4B   Choosing Rows 35
4B.1   Comparisons 35
4B.2   Ranges (BETWEEN) 36
4B.3   Lists (IN, NOT IN) 36

4B.4	Character string matches (LIKE, NOT LIKE)	36
4B.5	Unknown values (IS NULL, IS NOT NULL)	37
4B.6	Combinations of more than 1 argument (AND, OR)	37
4B.7	Negations (NOT)	38
4B.8	Eliminating duplicates (DISTINCT)	38

4 Expressions, Operators, Functions

4A Expressions

Most of the examples we have looked at selected data that is already there, extracting it directly from the database in the form in which it is stored

We performed some grouping and sorting. We now need to look at constructing data from the underlying information for inclusion in a query and also some of the ways that data can be filtered out so we are left with the information we want

In addition we need to understand how rows are chosen. It is therefore necessary to explore the concept of an expression (briefly looked at in section 1).

An expression consists of:
- a column name
- a constant
- a function
- a variable
- a subquery
- any combination of them

There is no theoretical limit to the length of an expression

They can be combined with operators.

The rule is that an expression returns a value or values (and can be nested).

They are used in many:
SQL statements,
- search conditions in WHERE and HAVING clauses
- select_lists (which cannot use every expression)
- ORDER BY clauses
- GROUP BY and HAVING clauses
- functions
- other expressions (or combinations of expressions)

Syntax overall:

    expression   operator   expression   operator   expression   etc

Syntax by component:

{constant | column_name | function | (subquery)} expression
[*{operator}*- operator
{constant | column_name | function | (subquery)}...] - expression
etc

Author's Notes:
- AND, OR and NOT are logical operators which are usually spelled out in the documentation instead of being included in the general description 'operators' so I have followed this approach here
- Much of the content of this section repeats the previous section on the select list.
- This is deliberate since it should be emphasized that expressions are of more general use (listed above)
- Operators are covered in separate sections and are subject to various rules of use

4A.1   Constants and Variables

4A.1a a *constant* is a literal value:

- numeric or character data (Character data must be enclosed within single quotation marks)
'Anything you might want to say'

Example:

see section 1A.8

4A.1b a *variable* identifier (in the form *variable_name*).

variables can be local or global.

Global variables can't be defined by users and are not used to pass information. They are called Global but are not server-wide
They are read only and return information about the current session
Example:

see section 1A.6

Local variables are declared first and then assigned a value
They are often used in batches of SQL statements, stored procedures and control-of-flow statement blocks
Their life is only that of the procedure in which they are declared.

Syntax:

DECLARE @variable_name datatype, @variable_name datatype . . .

Example:

see section 1A.4

In addition they are often used as counters for loops

4A.2   a *column_name* specifies a column.

4A.3   a function

refers to a built-in function (see the Functions topic)

4A.4 a subquery

is a nested SELECT statement (with some restrictions) that can be used in an expression (if it returns a single value)
(see the Subqueries topic later)

Example:
see section 1A.9

4A.2 Operators

4A.2a ARITHMETIC OPERATORS

Addition   (+)   )
Subtraction   (-)   )   can be used with numeric columns
Division   (/)   )
Multiplication (*)   )
Modulo   (%)   can only be used with int, smallint, and tinyint columns

When you run an arithmetic operation on a column whose value
is NULL, the result is NULL.

Mixed-mode arithmetic means the datatypes are not equivalent.
In such cases the lower type is converted to the higher type
(except that money always takes precedence).
Run Example 4 for the hierarchy contained in the
master.systypes system table.

When there is more than one arithmetic operator in an expression,
multiplication, division, and modulo are calculated first,
followed by subtraction and addition.

When all arithmetic operators in an expression have the same
level of precedence, the order of execution is left to right.

Expressions within parentheses take precedence over all other operations.

Examples:

1 To illustrate a simple calculated column (with headings)

   SELECT 'Number sold' = ytd_sales,
          'Price' = price,
          'Sales' = (ytd_sales * price),
           title
   FROM titles

2 A repeat of the earlier example to illustrate a complex constructed column

   SELECT Sales = ytd_sales * price,
    'To Author' = (ytd_sales * price * royalty)/100,
    'To Publisher' = ytd_sales * price - (ytd_sales * price * royalty)/100
   FROM titles

3 To illustrate the use of Modulo to round results to a complete 1,000

   SELECT 'Sales to complete 1,000' = (ytd_sales - ytd_sales % 1000),
           'Title' = title
   FROM titles

4 Datatype precedence from master.systypes

   USE master
   GO
   SELECT   name, type
   FROM   systypes
   ORDER BY   type

2B.1b LOGICAL OPERATORS - AND, OR, NOT

The logical operators AND, OR, and NOT are used to connect search conditions in where clauses.

AND joins two or more conditions and returns results only when <u>all</u> of the conditions are true.

Example:
```
SELECT      *
FROM        authors
WHERE       au_lname = 'Ringer'
AND         au_fname = 'Anne'
```

OR also connects two or more conditions, but it returns results when <u>any</u> of the conditions are true.

Example:
```
SELECT      *
FROM        authors
WHERE       au_fname = 'Anne'
OR          au_fname = 'Ann'
```

NOT <u>negates</u> the expression that follows it.

Example:
```
SELECT      *
FROM        authors
WHERE NOT   state = "CA"
```

When more than one logical operator is used in a statement, NOT is evaluated first, then AND, and finally OR

Note: OR and NOT are not 'true' search arguements since they use an alternative or a negative logic. Table scans are forced when you use NOT, so do not use it unless there is no other way.

2B.2 BITWISE OPERATORS

Bitwise operators perform mathematical operations between integer values (as translated to binary expressions within T-SQL statements)

All bitwise operators translate the integer parameters into binary representation before evaluating them

The bitwise operators are:

Symbol	Meaning	Can be used on
&	Bitwise AND	*int*, *smallint*, or *tinyint* columns only
|	Bitwise OR	*int*, *smallint*, or *tinyint* columns only
^	Bitwise exclusive OR	*int*, *smallint*, or *tinyint* columns only
~	Bitwise NOT	*int*, *smallint*, *tinyint*, or *bit* columns only

Example:

SELECT 17 & 11 = 1

```
calculation:   17  10001
               11  01011
                1  00001
```

Notice: a bitwise AND returns a 1 if both bits are set to 1

2B.3 COMPARISON OPERATORS

Comparison operators contrast a specific difference between two expressions

Comparisons must only be made between variables, columns, and so on, of similar type

In comparing *char* and *varchar* data
> < means closer to the beginning of the alphabet and
> > means closer to the end of the alphabet

In the ASCII collating sequence
> lowercase letters are greater than uppercase letters, and
> uppercase letters are greater than numbers

When comparing dates, < means earlier and > means later

Place quotation marks around all character and *datetime* data used with a comparison operator

Operator	Meaning
=	Equal to
>	Greater than
<	Less than
>=	Greater than or equal to
<=	Less than or equal to
< >	Not equal to
!>	Not greater than
!<	Not less than

Note: beware of negative logic when using the <> !> and !<

Examples:

```
SELECT   * FROM titleauthor
WHERE    royaltyper < 50


SELECT   authors.au_lname, authors.au_fname
FROM     authors
WHERE    au_lname >'McBadden'


SELECT   au_id, phone
FROM     authors
WHERE    phone !='415 658-9932'
```

Chapter 4 -Select Plus

```
SELECT   title_id,
         newprice = price * $1.15
FROM     pubs2..titles
WHERE    advance > 5000


SELECT   *
FROM     sales
WHERE    ord_date > '9/13/94'
```

2B.4 JOIN OPERATORS

Join operators compare two or more tables (or views) by:
1. specifying at least a column from each
2. comparing the values in those columns row by row
3. concatenating the rows for which the comparison is true

Comparisons must only be made between variables, columns, and so on, of similar type

Example - a join:

    SELECT   title, pub_name
    FROM   titles, publishers
    WHERE   titles.pub_id = publishers.pub_id

Joins that preserve **all** rows from a table in the results set, regardless of whether there is a matching row in the table to which they're being joined (*= and =*), are called outer joins

It is recommended that you use the ANSI-standard join clauses:
    JOIN (usually the word 'INNER' from INNER JOIN is omitted as it is implied)
    LEFT OUTER JOIN
    RIGHT OUTER JOIN
    FULL OUTER JOIN

Example - a join (new sybtax):

    SELECT   title, pub_name
    FROM   titles
    JOIN   publishers
    ON   titles.pub_id = publishers.pub_id

OUTER join operators:

Symbol	Meaning
*=	Include in the results all rows from the first table that meet the statement's restrictions. The second table returns values if there is a match on the join condition. Otherwise, the second table generates null values.
=*	The same but with the 'sides' reversed

Future versions of SQL Server may discontinue support for the "*=" and "=*" outer join operators

Example of an OUTER JOIN:
```
SELECT      t.title_id, sum(qty)
FROM        titles t, sales s
WHERE       t.title_id *= s.title_id
GROUP BY    t.title_id
```

New OUTER JOIN syntax:
```
SELECT            t.title_id, sum(qty)
FROM              titles t
LEFT OUTER JOIN   sales s
ON                t.title_id = s.title_id
GROUP BY          t.title_id
```

Null values in tables or views being joined will never match each other

Since *bit* columns do not permit null values, a value of 0 appears in an outer join when there is no match for a *bit* column in the inner table

Joins cannot be used for columns containing *text* or *image* values

Note: Joins will be revisited in the following Chapter

2B.5 STRING OPERATORS

String concatenation is allowed using the + symbol
All other string manipulation is handled through String Functions

The empty string ("") is not interpreted as a blank

In concatenating varchar, char or text data, use a single blank
    to join words as two words
        e.g. 'abc' + " " + 'def' is stored as 'abc def'

Example:
    SELECT 'abc' + ' ' + 'def'

2B.6 OPERATOR PRECEDENCE

When multiple operators are combined, operator precedence becomes an issue

Operator precedence determines the order in which computations or comparisons are performed

Operators have the following precedence level:

primary grouping	( )
bitwise	~
multiplicative	* / %
additive	+ -
bitwise	^
bitwise	&
bitwise	|
NOT	NOT
AND	AND
OR	OR

When all operators in an expression are of the same level, the precedence order is from left to right

You can change the order of execution with parentheses because primary grouping takes precedence and the most deeply nested expression evaluated first

Example: SELECT (10 + 4) - 7 * 3 / 2

Chapter 4 -Select Plus

4A.3   Functions

4A.3a Numeric Functions

4A.3a.1 Numeric Mathematical Functions

Syntax:
   SELECT function_name(parameters)

Note:
   Monetary type consist of decimal data in currency
   If there is no $ sign it is treated as numeric with 4 places of decimals
   Monetary values do not return values formatted with the dollar sign

   Floating point constants can be entered as decimal values
      or in exponential notation

Functions:	Parameters	Results
ABS	(numeric_expr)	Absolute
ACOS, ASIN,	(float_expr)	Angle in Radians
ATAN, ATN2	(float_expr)	Angle in Radians
COS, SIN	(float_expr)	Trig value in Radians
COT, TAN	(float_expr)	Trig value in Radians
CEILING	(numeric_expr)	Smallest Integer > value
DEGREES	(numeric_expr)	Conversion of Radians to Degrees
EXP	(float_expr)	Exponential
FLOOR	(numeric_expr)	Largest Integer <= value
LOG	(float_expr)	Natural Logarithm
LOG10	(float_expr)	Base 10 Logarithm
PI	( )	3.14159etc
POWER	(numeric_expr)	Value of numeric_expr to power of y
RADIANS	(numeric_expr)	Conversion of Degrees to Radians
RAND	(seed)	Random float between 0 and 1

ROUND	(numeric_expr)	Numeric_expr rounded to length specified
SIGN	(numeric_expr)	positive, negative, zero
SQRT	(float_expr)	Square root

Example:
```
SELECT FLOOR(123.45)       = 123
SELECT FLOOR($123.45)      = 123.00

SELECT CEILING( 123.45)    = 124

SELECT ROUND(123.4545, 2)  = 123.4500
SELECT ROUND(123.45, -2)   = 100.00
```

With the ROUND function, the last digit is always an estimate:
```
ROUND(123.9994, 3)         = 123.9990
ROUND(123.9995, 3)         = 124.0000
```

4A.3a.2   Numeric Aggregate Functions

Aggregate functions calculate summary values (per the following list)
from the values in a particular column, and returns a single value for
each set of rows to which the function applies

AVG Returns the average of all the values
or only the DISTINCT values, in the *expression*
AVG can be used only with numeric columns

COUNT Returns the number of non-null values in the *expression*.
When DISTINCT is specified, COUNT finds the number of
unique non-null values
including both numeric and character columns

COUNT(*) Returns the number of rows. COUNT(*)
takes no parameters
and cannot be used with DISTINCT.
All rows are counted, even those with null values.

MIN and MAX Returns the minimum or maximum value in the *expression*
MIN and MAX can only be used with:
- numeric
- character, and
- *datetime* columns
With character columns, MAX finds the highest value
in the collating sequence.
DISTINCT is available for ANSI compatibility
but it is not meaningful with MAX.

SUM Returns the sum of all the values
or only the DISTINCT values, in the *expression*
SUM can be used with numeric columns only

Except for COUNT(*), NULL rows are ignored

Syntax:
aggregate_ function ([ALL | DISTINCT] *expression*)

Example:
```
SELECT      AVG(advance), SUM(ytd_sales)
FROM  titles
WHERE       type = 'business'
```

When mixing datatypes, (e.g. summing *tinyint* and *int* values)
   use a resulting variable that will encompass both types

When you sum or average numeric data, Transact-SQL promotes the resulting datatype
   to the minimum precision and scale necessary to hold the result

In reports, the results of aggregate functions are shown as new columns

An aggregate may not appear in a WHERE clause, unless it is also included in:
   - the SELECT list
   - a subquery containing a HAVING clause

Aggregate functions often appear with GROUP BY
   which partitions a table into groups

These functions calculate a single value for each group

Without GROUP BY, an aggregate function in the select list
   produces a single value as a result
   whether it is operating on all the rows in a table
   or on a subset of rows defined by a WHERE clause

scalar aggregate function (single)
Aggregate functions, which calculate summary values from the non-null
   values in a particular column, can be applied to all rows in a table
In this case, they produce **a single aggregate value** called a *scalar aggregate function*

vector aggregate function (group)
Or they can be applied to all rows that have the same value in a column
   or columns or expression (with the GROUP BY and, optionally,
   the HAVING clause). In this case, they produce an **aggregate value for each group,** called a *vector aggregate function*

Performance tip: To avoid overflow errors, declare all variables that will hold the result of a sum or average with the most precise datatype of the values supplied

Examples:

SUM and AVG Function with a GROUP BY Clause
When used with a GROUP BY clause, aggregate functions produce single values for each group, rather than for the whole table

Summary values for each type of book:

```
SELECT      type,
            AVG(advance),
            SUM(ytd_sales)
FROM        titles
GROUP BY    type
```

COUNT of DISTINCT
Find the number of different cities in which authors live:

```
SELECT      COUNT(DISTINCT city)
FROM        authors
```

GROUP BY HAVING COUNT(*)
List the types in the *titles* table for books that have only one copy in inventory:

```
SELECT      type
FROM        titles
GROUP BY    type
HAVING      COUNT(*) = 1
```

HAVING SUM and AVG
Group the *titles* table by publisher and includes only groups of publishers who have paid more than $25,000 in total advances:

```
SELECT      pub_id, SUM(advance)
FROM        titles
GROUP BY    pub_id
HAVING      SUM(advance) > $25000
```

4A.3b String Functions (or Character functions)

General syntax:

function_name(character expression)

Note: if a string is used for the character expression it must be in quotes

Consist of any combination of letters, symbols and numbers

Most string functions can be used on char and varchar

Function   **Parameters and result**

+   (e.g. expression + expression) Concatenates

ASCII("char_expr")   ASCII code of leftmost character

CHAR(integer_expr) Char equivalent of ASCII value

CHARINDEX('pattern', expression)
            Returns to the starting position of the specified pattern

DIFFERENCE(char_expr1, char_expr)
            Evaluates the similarity of 2 expressions

LOWER(char_expr)   Converts to lower case

LTRIM(char_expr) Data without leading blanks

PATINDEX('%pattern%', expression)
            Returns the starting position of the first occurrence of 'pattern' in the specified string or a zero

REPLICATE(char_expr1, integer_expr)
            Repeats a character a specified number of times
    Example: SELECT REPLICATE('~',30)

REVERSE(char_expr) Returns the reverse of a character expression

RIGHT(char_expr1, integer_expr)
    Part of a char expression starting integer_expr from right

RTRIM(char_expr)   Data without trailing blanks

SOUNDEX(char_expr)   Returns a 4 digit SOUNDEX code to evaluate
                                the similarity of 2 char strings

SPACE(integer_expr)   Returns a string of repeated spaces

STR(float_expr[,length[,dec]])
    Returns char data converted from numeric data

(length = total length incl dec point, sign, digits
and spaces. dec = number of decimal places)

STUFF(char_expr1, start, length, char_expr2)
Deletes length characters from char_expr1 at start & then inserts
char_expr2 into char_expr1 at start

SUBSTRING   (expression, start, length)
Returns part of a character string

UPPER(char_expr)   Converts to upper case

Note: functions can be nested
Example: RTRIM(LTRIM(SUBSTRING(expression, start, length)))

Note:
Functions can be nested
Example:
SUBSTRING(RTIM(LTRIM(expression, start, length)))

Note 2: Character strings in character expressions must be enclosed in quotes

Chapter 4 -Select Plus

4A.3c Datetime Data

Date functions can be used in:
- the select_list
- the WHERE clause
- wherever an expression is used

Enclose Datetime values in quotes (single or double)

Some functions take a "date part" parameter
e.g. year, month, day, hour, second

Function Parameters   Results

DATEADD   (datepart, number, date)   Adds the number of dataparts to the date

DATEDIFF   (datepart, date1, date2)   Number of dataparts between two dates

DATENAME   (datepart, date)   Specified datepart for the listed date,
                               returned as an ASCII value (e.g. July)

DATEPART   (datepart, date)   Specified datepart for the listed date,
                               returned as an integer value (e.g. 7)

GETDATE   ( ) Current date and time in internal format

Datepart	Abbreviation	Values
year	yy	1753-9999
quarter	qq	1-4
month	mm	1-12
day of the year	dy	1-366
day	dd	1-31
week	wk	0-51
weekday	dw	1-7 (1 is Sunday)
hour	hh	0-23
minute	mi	0-59
second	ss	0-59
millesecond	ms	0-999

Examples:

    SELECT   title_id,
                    pubdate,
                    "PubDate +30 Days" = DATEADD(DAY, 30, pubdate)
    FROM   titles

    SELECT   "Yesterday ",
                    DATEADD(DAY, -1, GETDATE( ))

    SELECT   "This is the momth of ",
                    DATENAME(MONTH,GETDATE( ))

    SELECT   DATEDIFF(dd, "1/1/1900", getdate())

Note: the format of the date you enter must be a compatible format and be enclosed in quotes

Examples: "Jan 1 1990"
                    '3/3/84'
    SELECT * FROM titles WHERE pubdate > "1/1/93"

4A.3d System Functions

4A.3d.1 System tables

A shorthand method for querying system tables

Syntax: SELECT function_name(parameters)

Example:
    to query who is using the database -
    SELECT 'database' = db_name(), 'user' = user_name(), login = user_name()

Function	Parameters	Returns
COALESCE	(expr1, expr2, ...exprN)	first non-null result from the alternative columns listed
COL_NAME	(table_id, column_id)	column name
COL_LENGTH	('table_name', 'column_name')	col length
DATALENGTH	('expr')	actual length of expr
DB_ID	(database_id)	DB id
DB_NAME	('databasename')	DB name
GETANSINULL	('databasename')	default nullability for the db
HOST_ID	( )	host process id
HOST_NAME	( )	host computer name
IDENT_INCR	('table_name')	increment value for value specified during creation of an identity seed identity column
IDENT_SEED	('table_name')	seed value specified during creation of an identity column
INDEX_COL	('table_name', index_id, key_id)	indexed column name
ISNULL	(expr, value)	specified value in place of NULL
NULLIF	(expr1, expr2)	NULL if expr1 = expr2 specifies a NULL in place of a value
OBJECT_ID	(object_id)	db object id number
OBJECT_NAME	('object_name')	db object name
STATS_DATE	(table_id, index_id)	the last date the index statistics were updated for a database object
STATS_DATE	(table_name, index_name)	alternative to previous
SUSER_ID	(server_user_id)	SQL Server users id
SUSER_NAME	('server_username')	SQL Server user's name
USER_ID	(user_id)	users id

USER_NAME   ('username')   user's name

Example:
>
> | SELECT | length = datalength(pub_name), |
> |--------|-------------------------------|
> | | pub_name |
> | FROM | publishers |

4A.3d.2   Niladic Functions

These are System-supplied data that take no parameters which can be inserted into tables as default constraints

>   Current_timestamp
>   Current_user
>   Session_user
>   System_user
>   User

4A.3e Datatype Conversion

Enables:
- *conversion from one date type to another*
- *various formats*

CONVERT functions can be used in:
- the select_list
- the WHERE clause
- wherever an expression is used

Syntax:

CONVERT(datatype(length),expression,style)

Examples:

   1   SELECT   CONVERT (char(30), getdate(), 102)
Note: the number 102 refers to the format of the date

   2   SELECT   'Title Code' = pub_id +
                      UPPER(SUBSTRING(type,1,3))+
                      SUBSTRING(CONVERT(CHAR(4),
                      DATEPART(YY,pubdate)),3,2)
       FROM   titles

This query generates a contrived key code that consists of:
- the pub_id,
- the first three letters of the booktype (in Upper Case) and
- the last 2 digits of a four digit year

The values are converted first so that they can be concatenated to the other character strings

   3   SELECT   STR(1234567)

will convert the numeric to a string

## 4A.3f	Text and Image Functions

These functions are not covered in this introductory book
- PATINDEX
- SET TEXTSIZE
- TEXTPTR
- TEXTVALID

4B Choosing Rows

- meaning returning/selecting specific rows, as described in the WHERE clause.

Searching is done by basing the search on SARGs - Search Arguements

SARGs are expressions connected by search conditions - including:

1. Comparison operators   = > < >= <= <> != !< !=

2. Ranges   BETWEEN and NOT BETWEEN

3. Lists   IN and NOT IN

4. String matches   LIKE and NOT LIKE

5. Unknown values   IS NULL and IS NOT NULL

6. Combinations of these   AND and OR

7. Negations   NOT

Note: The NOT conditions are not recognized by the query optimizer and therefore force a table scan. The impact of this on a large table has to be seen to be believed, we are talking many many orders of magnitude of time

4B.1 Example based on a comparison:

Arithmetic operators are used for comparisons, including:

>   =
>   <
>   >
>   >=
>   <=
>   !>
>   !<
>   ( ) precedence control
>   <> NOT equal to (watch the optimizer, whenever
>   negative logic is used a table scan results)

Note:

Use single quotations round char, varchar and smalldatetime columns
 – you **can** use double quotes (")
  but the ANSI standard is single quotes (')

Example:
```
SELECT      *
FROM        authors
WHERE       zip > '90000'
```

4B.2 Example based on a range (BETWEEN):

the BETWEEN and AND keywords enable the use of ranges
 BETWEEN is a range start keyword
 AND is a range end keyword
the end-points of the between are included in the selection

Example:
```
SELECT      pubdate, title
FROM        titles
WHERE       pubdate BETWEEN '1/1/91' AND '12/31/91'
```

Example based on a range and a comparison:
```
SELECT      pubdate, title, price
FROM        titles
WHERE       pubdate BETWEEN '1/1/91' AND '12/31/91'
AND         price > 10.00
```

4A.3 Example based on a list (IN):

the IN keyword enables the use of lists

Example:
```
SELECT      title, type
FROM        titles
WHERE       type IN ('mod_cook', 'trad_cook')
```

4B.4 Example based on a character string (LIKE):

The LIKE keyword selects rows containing columns that match specified portions of character strings

Strings can be used with an Arithmetic operator in the same manner as numbers – SQL Server uses the ANSI order for comparisons.
i.e. any lower case character is less than the upper case character no matter where it is in the alphabet.

The LIKE keyword takes 4 wildcard characters:

%	(percent)	any string of characters
_	(underscore)	any single character
[ ]	(square brackets)	any single character within the specified range
^	(caret)	any single character not within the specified range

A string must always be enclosed in quotation marks
– use double quotes "string"

A string containing quotation marks must be enclose in quotes. The convention is to use double quotes on the outer definition and single quotes inside

Chapter 4 -Select Plus

Example:
> SELECT "The string's the thing"

Example	Definition
LIKE AB%	beginning with AB
LIKE 'Ab%'	beginning with Ab
LIKE %een	ending with een
LIKE '%en%'	with en in it
LIKE'_en'	3 letter words ending in en
LIKE '[CK]%'	begins with C or K
LIKE '[S V]ing'	begins with letter from S to V
LIKE 'M[^c]%'	beginning with M and not having c as the second letter

Example based on character string

```
SELECT    stor_name
FROM      stores
WHERE     stor_name LIKE '%Book%'
```

4B.5 Example based on unknown Values

i.e. the user did not enter a value i.e. a NULL or NOT NULL
a NULL means no value entered – it is NOT equivalent to a zero or a blank

NULL fails all comparisons and cannot be equal to each other

NULL sorts low – will always be first in an ascending sorted result

SELECT	title
FROM	titles
WHERE	price IS NULL

4B.6 Example based on several arguments

Using logical operators – AND, OR and NOT in the WHERE clause
    enables the combination of arguments
This must be used with caution,
    NOT forces a table scan because the optimizer does not recognize it
The order of evaluation of logical arguments is:
    1 NOT
    2 AND
    3 OR
    but parens can be used to change this
Arithmetical operators are evaluated before logical

Examples:

SELECT	title_id, title, pub_id, price, pubdate
FROM	titles
WHERE	(title LIKE 'T%' OR pub_id = '0877')
AND	(price > 16.00)

SELECT	title_id, title, pub_id, price, pubdate
FROM	titles
WHERE	(title LIKE 'T%')
OR	pub_id = '0877'
AND	(price > 16.00)

SELECT	title_id, title, pub_id, price, pubdate
FROM	titles
WHERE	title LIKE 'T%'
OR	pub_id = '0877'
AND	(price > 16.00)

4B.7 Negations

In general the word NOT means the opposite and is intuitively obvious as to its meaning but the negative logic can become like trying to follow what someone is saying when they are using double negatives in speech

NOT Example:
I know that what you did not hear is not what you thought I said but what you thought you heard is not what I meant
E.G. IF NOT EXISTS

This is easy to follow when not wrapped up other logic but as soon as the logic gets beyond a simple statement it can become a nightmare

Example of NOT:

> **SELECT   title**
> **FROM   titles**
> **WHERE   price IS NOT NULL**

If you try to find rows with a NULL value in a column that has been defined as NOT NULL query you will get an error

Examples:

> **NOT BETWEEN**
> **NOT IN**
> **NOT LIKE**
> **<>** (means NOT EQUAL)
> **NOT NULL**

It is often possible to re-write a query that will use other methods of choosing rows:

e.g.   Instead of:
> **NOT BETWEEN 10 AND 20**

use
> **>= 10 AND <= 20**

4B.8 Eliminating duplicates (DISTINCT)

The DISTINCT keyword enables the elimination of duplicates

This applies to the whole select_list
– only unique combinations of the select_list are included in the result set
You cannot use DISTINCT on one column only – only the whole selection

    SELECT DISTINCT   **city, state**
    FROM   **authors**

This yields the unique cases of the city and state combination (being Distinct)
i.e. this query operates on the whole row of the result set
(see also section 1A earlier in this chapter)

Chapter 5 - Tips

TIPS FOR WORKING IN THE SSMS

So you now have some knowledge of SQL server, T-SQL and using Management Studio.

It is time for forming good habits.

This chapter will attempt to start you off in the right direction. While rules are meant to be broken etc. – much pain and suffering can be avoided if you start with good habits and develop your own style and approach once you have progressed

"Oh, it's Ok, I learn from my mistakes." A radio talk-show host once said (I forget who) that the man who learns from his mistakes is an idiot. The wise man learns from the mistakes of others and then avoids them

There is nothing special about these tips – they will help but then you may already know them. Anyway maybe you would like to read them as suggestions to be adopted or discarded. Personally I have found them extremely useful. Can they be improved upon?

Probably! – email me with any suggestions you have.

Final Note before you get into this chapter: This chapter is put here so that you can scan them at this stage. You will not understand them all but you can come back again – and again.

Heads up – I am using the following shorthand instructions
RtClk meaning Right Click,
1xClk meaning Single Click and
2xClk to mean Double Click (the mouse)

Chapter 5:
Outline = The Context Tool

5.1	Start with Use DB GO
5.2	Highlight code and execute
5.3	Comment-bracket subsidiary code in the window pane
5.4	Copy/Paste – don't type names
5.5	Build-up queries
5.6	Query results to Grid, File, Text and why
5.7	Save query code to File>>Save SQL query as
5.8	Develop a Style
5.9	F5 - Execute
5.10	Copy result set to clipboard
5.11	Run a harmless query before DML code
5.12	Establish a war-chest of your own
5.13	Learn to search the iNet
5.14	Don't play in the ProdDB
5.15	Backup according to a plan and test restores
5.16	Start View and SP names with a number so they are listed first
5.17	Always write comments in your SPs
5.18	Use a naming convention
5.19	Use intuitive names – avoid abbreviations but don't be rediculous about it
5.20	Set Tools>>Options
5.21	Alter your recent file limit to Max which is 24
5.22	Set up a folder for your query results – expand this to a folder structure
5.23	Use Query Option = Results to Text to list your Column names
5.24	Use WHERE 1 = 2 to get headings only
5.25	Learn shortcuts
5.27	Intellisense
5.28	Copy with headers
5.29	Niladic function
5.30	Use Environment\Keyboard to set you own shortcuts

5.31   When writing SPs use a DROP statement commented out
5.32   Intelligent aliases in code not a b etc
5.33   Consider including DB name in result sets
5.34   Don't BU to tape
5.35   Establish BU plan ASAP
5.36   Copy 2xClk Word
5.37   Start selection item with a ,
5.38   Learn to Detach and Attach DB
5.39   Call a SP that you have written to perform routine tesks
5.40   Copy a Name form the Object Explorer pane
5.41   Develop your own techniques for increasing readability

5.1 Start with Use DB

Get into the habit of starting your code with the instruction of which database to address. This ensures you are in the right place.

Syntax:
   USE database_name
      GO

GO: Separate SQL statement clusters with the separator GO.

Example:
   USE pubs
      GO

5.2 Highlight code and execute

This is a very powerful technique. It enables you to work on various code sections in the same pane.
You can write DML code inside a Comment and still execute it by this technique.
However, you can leave SELECT code that you use in the current exercise out of 'Comment' so that it is the default code that executes when you F5

5.3 Comment-bracket subsidiary code in the window pane

This guards against inadvertantly running code you did not mean. I always put my UPDATE code in comment boundary markers /* */ so that it never gets run until I positively run it by highlighting and executing it

I do not delete colum names but rather use '- -' to comment them out if I think I might use them later

5.4 Copy/Paste – don't type names

Typos happen – copy/paste avoids them. 2xClk (Double click) to select a field name or word, Ctrl-C to copy then 2xClk to select, Ctrl-V to paste

5.5 Build-up queries
Test as you go. Start with the simplest query and develop it in stages.
When coding complex JOINs you might want to run a SELECT on each table first to get the column names correct.

5.6 Query results to Grid, File, Text and why
You can use Ctrl-D to return the results of a query in a Grid
You can use Ctrl-Shft- F to return the results of a query to a file – you will be prompted for a filename
You can use Ctrl-T to return the results of a query as Text
Use the Text option to copy column headings (2xClk) each heading or highlight the whole heading row by dragging the cursor from the top of the heading row ro the bottom of the heading row – this highlights the row the Ctrl-C
You can also use Home to move to the beginning of the row and then Shft-End to highlight the heading row
Copy then Paste the heading row into the code pane. Of course there are millions of spaces to get rid of.

5.7 Save code to File>>Save SQL query as
Queries get stored as active files as you write each query. When you quit SSMS you are asked if you want to save the active TAB panes.
As a long-term library, you can establish a folder and save your queries there for future reference.

Why would you want to do this? Well, you might want to have an electronic record of what you have done. For example, consider when you change options or setup for your applications. The problem with doing this in the GUI is that you cannot print it out. Screenshots are a good technique. Saving your code is another.

5.8 Develop a Style
Indenting code is essential to easily reading it. The code pane contributes to easy reading with color coding Keywords (Blue) and text (Red), Comments are green. This helps.

USE upper case for Keywords and Proper case for Tablenames and Column names

5.9 F5
There are 6 ways to execute code in SSMS:

1.	Icon	**1xClk Execute icon**
2.	Menu	**Query>>Execute**
3.	RtClk	**RtClk >> Execute**
4.	Keyboard	**Ctrl-E**
5.	Keyboard	**F5**
6.	Keyboard	**Alt-X**

Depending on whether you prefer the mouse or the keyboard you might choose either the icon or F5.

(The others take milliseconds longer that might add up to 2.762876529871 weeks of your life over a 30 year period just clicking those extra keys or looking for the menu or ribbon icon choices – sic).

5.10 Copy result set to clipboard
Select the result set with Ctrl-A then RtClk on the grey cell at top of Row-heading column (or to the left of the Column-heading row) then RtClk and select form the menu.
You will find that you can include the headings or not)

5.11 Run a harmless query before DML code
Because a SELECT query is always harmless, run the appropriate SELECT before you run any DML code. In this way you can ensure that your query will access the data you intend – a long way towards the result being what you intended.

5.12 Establish a war-chest of your own
While it is not a good idea to save everything you ever did (this gets out of hand) establish a folder system (using Type of operation) to save query samples that you might need for later.

5.13 Learn to search the iNet

The internet (Google) can usually supply example code for almost anything you want to do. As you gain proficincy you will be able to discern the good from the Bad (or the Ugly) code.

5.14 Don't play in the ProdDB

Always practice or experiment in a test database. It is easy to backup a database and restore it with a new name for testing. This also tests your backup (that it does restore).

5.15 Backup according to a plan and test restores

Do not just accept defaults for names of backups. Develop a naming convension so you can identify the backup that you need when you come to restore. The date of the BU should be included also the name of the database and some indication of the status at that time.

For example: CXT2_2012_1212_B4-YrEndAdjustments

5.16 Start View and SP names with a number to top-list them

Numbers list before letters so start names with numbers and they will be listed at the top. This is useful when there are hundreds of SPs in a database and you need to find your SP. Also put you initials or name in the name so you know it was you that wrote it

For example:
[01_CliffSP_ECF_CurrentInvHoldgs_Rept]

While writing this – please use a '0' infront of the single digits so that your names sort into the correct order instead of 1, 11, 12, 2, 3 etc. Rather have 01, 02, 03, 11, 12

5.17 Always write comments in your SPs

To explain what the code does – but it can be used as a planning tool (write the comments 1st)

To exclude some of the code from execution – comment out field names instead of deleting them – you can then reinstate them easily

Comments are there for a number of reasons:
To guide developers who come along in the future
To remind you what you did when you come back to your code

You may find that you are judged ion the quality of you coding and comments are an integral part of code

5.18 Use a naming convention

Try to avoid abbreviations but not to such an extent that your names become unwieldy

Do NOT put 'tbl' or anything like it in fromt of a table name – we know it is a table. However, vw can go in front of a view name and sp or sproc in front of a SP

Use the underscore character to separate words in a name if it adds to the readability

Use Proper case in Table and Field names

Avoid name that mean nothing eg INM00300 (Yes, I know Microsoft does this but they bought the product from someone else)

Do not use prefixes in field names eg Customer table use fname, lname NOT cusfname cuslname cusaddress cusphone cusfax etc the context or table name will suffice

Eg dbo.Customers.fname

Exception ONLY use the table name in the ID column eg Customer table has a column CustomerID

Keep names as short as you can while still achieving readability – you may have to type them often

5.19 Use intuitive names – avoid abbreviations but don't be rediculous about it

Microsoft did not write Great Plains ERP. They said they would rewrite the code but in the last 10 years have not done that. The tables in the Great Plains ERP system have been described as ugly. The General Ledger module uses table name such as GL00100 etc. This does not help developers. Of course the manufacturer (if that is what we should call the owner of the system) does not want you to get into the system and will void their warrantee if you do. I had a case with the SalesLogix application that someone had done that and the warrantee was invalidated.

However the GP ERP system still uses a Logical Code for the table names and this is a common procedure. Usually a group of tables will use a convension like

GL   General Ledger module

00xxxx System setup options
10xxxx Unposted transactions
20xxxx Posted transactions
30xxxx Scoreboard tables – running balances
40xxxx History
50xxxx Definitions
60xxxx Temp tables

So again, a naming convension of sorts. You can go as far or as little as you like but you will have to use your own system in the future and possibly have employees that will also need to keep track. In systems of 1000+ tables this will get out of control unless you establish a system.
The naming system should include column as well as table names.
A part of the system may be to Use Proper case – but please do NOT use spaces in your names – that is what the underscore character is for.

Some advocates will say never abbreviate. Unfortunately we will all find 50 character tablenames unweildy and far too long – especially when printing code on letter-sized paper.

5.20 Set Tools>>Options

In Management Studio go to the menu item Tools>>Options. You can set such things as the time for Time-out and the TAB Stop distance. While you may just leave this alone for now it is as well to look at the items and know that you can set them to your preference. Be carefull that you do not get used to an alteration you have made and then go to another machine where your preference is not set.

5.21 Alter your recent file to Max (24)

In File >> Recent – there is a number (default is xx) – alter it to the Max number of files which is 24. Why would you not? Set this in Tools>>Options as in 5.20 above.

5.22 Set up a folder for your query results – expand this to a folder structure

Folders for results can be a good idea and even a whole structure. One of my recent contracts involved 12 companies – I set up 12 parent folders with 12 subfolders in each. These 144 folders enabled us to manage what we were doing efficiently. It is surprising how easy it is for things to get confusing so develop this good habit.

5.23 Use Query Option = Results to Text to list your Column names

When you want to type column names my advice is DON'T. Run a query
SELECT * FROM tablename after setting the Results to Text option (Ctrl-T). You can then 2xClk on the column heading and copy it. This saves many typo mistakes. (Notwithstanding Intellisense).

5.24 Use WHERE 1 = 2 to get headings only

If you just want the headings of a table there is no need to return all 20 million rows. An impossible WHERE clause will cause only the headings to be returned.
Of course you could use HWERE 1 > 2 or any other impossible WHERE clause

5.25 Learn shortcuts

F5	**Execute**
Alt-D	**Results to Grid**
Alt-T	**Results to Text**
Ctrl-Shft-F	**Results to File**

The usual Windows shortcuts work (Ctrl-C – Copy, Ctrl-V – Paste etc)
F8 to display the Object Explorer (you can then put it away and give yourself more room to code)

5.26 Include Statistics if you want to tune your query

If ever there was a Silver Bullet it is in the statistics. Minimize the number of pages read and you will minimise the time taken for a query to run. Time is also reported – you can use this as well – perhaps you need to run the query in 2 stages (or more) using temporary tables

Using this technique you can compare the effects of the order of execution in your queries

5.27 Intellisense

This is a great facility (but can be a pain also) – learn to use it wisely

For example, the get the name of the server you can type in SELECT @@ - at this point intellisense will list the Global Variable (designated by the @@) and a whole lot of other items for you to choose from. O fcourse you have to know to type in the @@ beginning or intellidense does not know what you are requiring

5.28 Copy with headers

The Grey cell at the top left (top of rows columns [OK so left of the Columns row] will select all the cells in the result set but if you RtClk on it you can choose Copy with Headers to the clipboard

5.29 Niladic functions

These are functions that return system data (e.g. DB_Name) and takes no arguments
"Nil" means nothing or null, and "adic" means arguments.

Niladic functions are functions with no parameters that should be specified without parentheses. For example, the SQL Server's store specific function CURRENT_TIMESTAMP is nilladic, where is NewID() is not.

Note that both have no parameters.

These niladic functions were actually introduced in prior versions.

Though these functions are redundant, it helps to know what a niladic function is and what it does--a question that sometimes pops up during interviews to gauge how well an applicant knows SQL Server.

The following niladic functions have been supported in SQL Server since version 6.0 but are still included to follow the ANSI 92 standard.

Each niladic function is equated with a newer function that accepts arguments

Legacy function	Current
USER	USER_NAME()
CURRENT_USER	USER_NAME()
SESSION_USER	USER_NAME()
SYSTEM_USER	SUSER_NAME()
CURRENT_TIMESTAMP	GETDATE()

These functions can be used in a variety of places.

Examples:

```
CREATE TABLE x
(
DateEntered1 datetime NOT NULL
        CONSTRAINT df1   DEFAULT CURRENT_TIMESTAMP,
DateEntered2 datetime NOT NULL
        CONSTRAINT df2   DEFAULT 'GETDATE()'
)

DECLARE @Sysuser1 varchar(20),  @Sysuser2 varchar(20)
SET @Sysuser1 = SYSTEM_USER
SET @Sysuser2 = SUSER_NAME()
```

5.30 Use Environment\Keyboard to set your own shortcuts

Menu item >> **Tools \ Options \ Keyboard** enables you to set your own keyboard shortcuts but, unfortunately, does not put the code into the Query pane. You can use the built-in-already shortcuts:

Alt-F1	sp-help
Ctrl-1	sp_who
Ctrl-2	sp-lock

5.31 When writing SPs use a DROP statement commented out

- - DROP PROC SP_Name
CREATE PROC SP_Name

Or you can merely use ALTER SP_Name

This will help with the development of your stored procedures because you can highlight the DROP PROC SP_Name and run it without altering any code (the comment '- - ' stays there; you just don't highlight it)

5.32 Intelligent aliases in code not a b etc

A table called a and a table called b – this does nothing for readability

Example: FROM Customers a, Vendors b

Instead use:

FROM	Customers	AS Cus
JOIN	Vendors	AS Ven
WHERE	Cus.ID = Ven.ID	

5.33 Consider including DB name in result sets

When returning a Report, consider bringing name of the database in the result set. This can minimise the confusion from a multiple database environment
You can do this by using SELECT DB_Name as one of your columns

5.34 Don't BU to tape
Here is a serious question – do you think you should restore from a tape?

5.35 Establish BU plan ASAP
One of the disasters I came across was a client who had not backed up because they were waiting until they finished loading the data. The data took 2 months to load and they ended up starting again. This is time consuming and costly. The rule is: 'start backing up as soon as you have something to lose' which may be after you finish installing the program.

Do not use the defaults – establish a naming system so that you can identify which backup you might want to restore. While there is a date of each backup, this may not be adequate, especially when you are loading data.

5.36 Copy 2xClk Word
Typos abound. Spelling mistakes occur. S happens so I is good practice to copy/paste instead of typing. Intellisense helps. So the process is:

>**2xClk the word**
>**Ctrl-C**
>**Select the destination (2xClk if you are replacing a word)**
>**Ctrl-V**

5.37 Start selection item with a , (Comma)
When developing queries, your SELECT list is separated by commas. Place the comma at the beginning of the following line instead of at the end of the line. This helps comment-out items (lines) in your query

Example:

SELECT fname
>**, laname**
>**, building**
>**, street**
>**, city**

A line can be commented out like this:
SELECT fname
>**, laname**

    - -, building
    , street
    , city

This saves fiddling with the commas when you want to exclude an item

5.38 Learn to Detach and Attach DB

To move a database:
1. Backup the database
2. Restore it with a new name – this makes a copy
3. Detach the database
4. Move it to where you want it
5. Attach the database to the new server

This can be done without worrying about security as long as you login to the server as sa with the appropriate password in both cases. (Note: The passwords can be different – it makes no difference as long as you have the authority to perform the task on THAT server)

5.39 Copy a Name from the Object Explorer pane

The name of a stored procedure or a view can be difficult to read.
    Highlight the name
    F2
    Ctrl-C
    Esc

5.40 Get the name of the server

    SELECT @@SERVERNAME

5.41 Develop your own techniques for enhancing readability

Firstly, this Tip only addresses the display (and not processing) issues. Processing issues are dealt with in a more advanced book. So for now let's look at the display of datetime data.

Example:
   Datetime is a pain but can be much more readable if you truncate the display to the leftmost (first) 11 characters

   CONVERT(CHAR(11),date)

This will return the date as a string (CHAR) and drop the time from the resultset.

New functions appear in SQL Server with each version. The following will work to return the date only part of datetime

   CONVERT(Date, tablename)

```
SELECT CONVERT(VARCHAR(10), GETDATE(), 111)
```

Use CONVERT to convert the format of the date returned

101	U.S.	mm/dd/yyyy
102	ANSI	yy.mm.dd
103	British/French	dd/mm/yyyy
110	USA	mm-dd-yy
111	JAPAN	yy/mm/dd
112	ISO	yymmdd
		yyyymmdd

When you convert to character data from smalldatetime, the styles that include seconds or milliseconds show zeros in these positions. You can truncate unwanted date parts when you convert from datetime or smalldatetime values by using an appropriate char or varchar data type length.

5.42 Write a UDF (User-defined Function)

If you find you have to use a CONVERT or CAST repeatedly, write yourself a function.

Pro – this can save you a lot of time
Con – this makes your code specific to you instead of being open

- this seems to make sense until you find that what may look like a datetime has already been converted in the database and is not a datetime. Using * will always bring back the data as it is defined in the table
- before you go rushing to implement such ideas realize that many pros in the field do not do this so just put it in your warchest and know how to do it

```
CREATE FUNCTION     dbo.Fn_DateOnly(@DateInput datetime)
RETURNS             varchar(10)
BEGIN
RETURN              CONVERT(varchar(10), @DateInput,101)
END
```

In your code you can now use SELECT dbo.Fn_DateOnly(ColumnName) as follows:

Example:

```
SELECT    stor_id
         , ord_num
         , dbo.Fn_DateOnly(ord_date)
         , qty
         , title_id
FROM      sales
```

5.43 What makes DateTime so difficult and complex?

SQL Server stores DateTime as 2 Four-byte integers and SmallDateTime as 2 Four-byte integers. This means that you will not be able to compare in the WHERE clause.

The short answer is to set the individual time parts to zero and maintain the datetime datatype.

This is best done in table CHECK Constraints when inputting data:
ALTER TABLE [dbo].[RM10101]
WITH CHECK
ADD CHECK
(

```
(datepart(hour,[POSTEDDT])=(0) AND
datepart(minute,[POSTEDDT])=(0) AND
datepart(second,[POSTEDDT])=(0) AND
datepart(millisecond,[POSTEDDT])=(0))
)
```

5.44 Using Table Aliases

Assigning a table alias can increase the readability and clarity of your queries.

Consider this Delete statement:
```
DELETE      titleauthor
WHERE       au_id IN
            (SELECT authors.au_id
            FROM   authors
            JOIN   titles
                   ON authors .au_id = titleauthur.au_id
            JOIN   titleauthur
                   ON titleauthor.title_id = titles.title_id
            WHERE titles.title     LIKE '%computers%)
```

Table aliasing results in:
```
DELETE      titleauthor
WHERE       au_id IN
            (SELECT   a.au_id
            FROM      authors a
            JOIN      titles t
              ON      a.au_id = ta.au_id
            JOIN      titleauthur ta
              ON      titleauthor.title_id = t.title_id
            WHERE     t.title
            LIKE      '%computers%)
```

However aliases can be assigned by using the AS keyword – like this:
```
DELETE      titleauthor
WHERE       au_id IN
            (SELECT a.au_id
            FROM    authors       AS a
            JOIN    titles        AS t
                ON a.au_id = ta.au_id
            JOIN    titleauthur   AS ta
                ON titleauthor.title_id = t.title_id
            WHERE   t.title       LIKE '%computers%)
```

Since the AS is optional, it is for you to decide whether to use it or not

5.45 Use a harmless query before a DML statement

When creating a statement that modifies data (Update or Delete) you should:

1   write a SELECT statement first
2   test that it returns the desired results
3   then create the statement

Chapter 6 - Joins

CHAPTER 6

Retrieving Data
- Continued

This module or chapter was originally called the Advanced section of data retrieval. It is, perhaps, the next step but I would hesitate to tell any student of T-SQL that the subjects covered in the chapter will catapult them into the realm of the 'advanced' developer. Each of the topics covered have to be completely mastered - it is inconceivable that any developer worthy of the name not be familiar with these techniques. So - there is nothing so called 'advanced' about this chapter except that you should have achieved familiarity with prior chapters before going on to chapter 6.

JOINS - The first topic is Joins. The concept of a join is fundamental to T-SQL and merely utilizes the opposite of the normalization process. A join is the reconstruction of data from the normalized form into a complete record (or, at least, a more complete record) once more.

One technique for constructing a join query in practice is to divide the required data into the tables that are to be accessed and use a SELECT statement against each table. This will 'prove' the names in the select_list and the tables from where they will come.

Note: you can run **SET ROWCOUNT 10** in isql/w to restrict the resultset to 10 rows (or whatever number of rows you want) so you do not have to deal with massive numbers of rows. Do not, at this stage, use a WHERE clause. Write each SELECT statement on the same query in the query pane then highlight the code you wish to run and F5 to run them individually.

Once you have run all the SELECT statements for all the required columns, cut and paste them together, in whatever order and combination is appropriate. It is very good practice to Copy/Paste rather than attempt to type in column names – it usually cuts down the error rate due to typos.

The filtering restrictions in a WHERE clause can then be applied to complete the requirements of the query.

SUBQUERIES - The technique is - divide and conquer. Get the subquery right first and insert it (by Copy/Paste) into the main query. Develop each separately and then assemble the working queries to produce the whole result.

UNION - this is just a concatenation technique for combining the results of queries into a single result set.

Chapter 6:
Retrieving Data
- Continued

This module is designed to enable you to:

1. Correlate summary data with joins
2. Write subqueries
3. Create result-set tables
4. Combine results with the UNION operator

Outline - Context Tool

1	**JOIN**	5
1A	The Rules	5
1B	Unrestricted Join	6
1C	Equijoins	6
1D	Natural Joins	7
1E	Joins with two or more tables	7
1F	Self Joins (within the same table)	8
1G	Outer Joins	9
1H	Theta Joins	10
2	**Subqueries**	11
2A	Nesting SELECT statements	12
2B	Types of subquery	12
2C	Subquery restrictions	14
2D	Correlated subqueries	15
3	**SELECT INTO statement**	16
4	**UNION operator**	17

6A JOIN

The method used to combine fields from two tables by using values common to each is called a JOIN.

In a query, a SQL JOIN clause combines records (Columns) from two or more tables in a database.

The resultset can be saved as a virtual table (View) or used as it is.

There are two methods or you can call them syntaxes available, ANSI and SQL Server. SQL Server will accept the ANSI Standard syntax as well as its own syntax and they can be interchanged

The ANSI standard SQL specifies four types of JOIN:

1. INNER,
2. OUTER,
3. LEFT, and
4. RIGHT.

As a special case, a table (base table, view, or joined table) can JOIN to itself in a self-join.

Tables are 'joined' by specifying a column containing data which
    is compared in each table (usually an equality)

The process compares the values in the columns row by row
    and **concatenates** rows where the comparison is true

SQL Server will use the most efficient way of referencing the tables
    e.g. the order of join references

A join is implemented by using the SELECT statement
    with a comparison in the WHERE clause

Note: join references are not the only entries in a WHERE clause,
    there are filters as well

6A.1 The Rules:

1   The select_list usually displays columns from >1 table

2   The FROM clause names all the tables involved in the join

3   The WHERE clause specifies which rows should be
      included in the result set
      (the join operator is used in the WHERE clause)

4   Non-selected columns can still be referenced elsewhere in the query

5   Generally, to construct a joined record, a Primary key is
      equated(matched 1-1 or 1-n) with a Foreign key

6   Join operators other than an equality may be used to test
      column values as a method of choosing rows (see Theta joins)

6A.2 Unrestricted JOINS (a.k.a. Cross Join)

Includes two or more tables **without** a WHERE clause

Returns an unusable result set (the Cartesian Product of the tables)
    nevertheless this step is, conceptually, the first in processing a join
    (WHERE clause filters the result set returned)

Syntax:
    SELECT   select_list
    FROM   table_list

Example:
    SELECT   pub_name, title
    FROM   titles, publishers

(you should get 144 rows being 8 * 18 rows)
Also, the following ANSI syntax will work:

Example:
    SELECT   pub_name, title
    FROM   titles CROSS JOIN publishers

This informs anyone reading your code that you meant to do it.

How joins are processed

It is important to understand how SQL Server processes a join
    in order to know how to structure a query for efficiency

1   form the cartesian product of the tables as defined in
           the FROM clause and SELECT statement

2   apply the filter formed by the WHERE clause
           i.e. eliminate the results that do not satisfy the WHERE clause
           from the denormalized results in the cartesian result set

This method will attain much greater significance as we look at
    subsequent sections on joins and optimization, so visualize
    the method and understand it.

6A.3 Equijoins

An equijoin chooses ALL the columns from both tables where there is a match between that satisfies the join operator (including the redundant columns)

Syntax:
SELECT	select_list (includes all the columns)
FROM	table_list
WHERE	column, operator, column

Example:
SELECT	*
FROM	authors, publishers
WHERE	authors.city = publishers.city

Note: the 'all columns' choice produces redundant column data (city & state) which are common to both tables

So an Equijoin is not usually used since it produces redundant data in the resultset (see Natural Joins below)

6A.4 Natural Joins

A natural join eliminates redundant column data in the result set

A natural join is an equijoin with the redundant join columns removed

Example:
SELECT	publishers.pub_id, publishers.pub_name, authors.*
FROM	publishers, authors
WHERE	publishers.city = authors.city

Note: this eliminates redundant column data (city & state)
i.e. we have chosen all the columns from the *authors* table but only certain columns from the *publishers* table

6A.5 JOINS with more than two tables

You join more than 2 tables by specifying at least n-1 join clauses
where n is the number of tables joined

Although there is no limit to the number of tables, there can be a practical limit, depending upon the design of the database

There are two syntaxes available ANSI and SQL Server T-SQL which may be called Explicit and Implicit

SQL Server syntax – Implicit:

Syntax:

```
SELECT      select_list
FROM        table_list
WHERE       column, operator, column
AND         column, operator, column
```

Example:

```
SELECT      stor_name, qty, title
FROM        titles, stores, sales
WHERE       titles.title_id = sales.title_id
AND         stores.stor_id = sales.stor_id
```

SQL Server allows the join clause to be expressed in the WHERE clause along with the restrictive filters

ANSI syntax – Explicit:

Syntax:

```
SELECT   select_list
FROM     table_01
JOIN     table_02 ON   table_01.column, operator, table_02.column
JOIN     table_03 ON   table_01.column, operator, table_03.column
```

Example:

```
SELECT      stor_name,
            qty,
            title
FROM        titles
JOIN sales  ON    titles.title_id = sales.title_id
JOIN stores ON    stores.stor_id = sales.stor_id
```

6A.5a Aliasing table names in JOINS

Aliasing can really add to the readability of a query by applying a shorthand (abbreviations) to table names

Let's look at the last example aliasing the table names. Whenever a table name is dpecified in the FROM (including JOIN) clause we will assign an alias and substitute this abbreviation or alias whenever we refer to it in the future.

Example:

```
SELECT        stor_name, qty, title
FROM          titles  t1
JOIN sales t2  ON    t1.title_id = t2.title_id
JOIN stores t3 ON    t3.stor_id = t2.stor_id
```

Now, personally, I find this somewhat confusing so I have always used a more intuitive abbreviation, such as sal for sales, t can be used for titles because there is one one of them and st for stores:

Example:

```
SELECT         stor_name, qty, title
FROM           titles  t
JOIN sales sal  ON    t.title_id = sal.title_id
JOIN stores st  ON    st.stor_id = sal.stor_id
```

ALSO we have only used column names that have no ambiguity because they occur in only one table. There is only one stor_name in all three tables – the same as qty and title BUT what happens when there is two or more of the same column names such as title_id (we may want the title_id in our resultset). We have to use the either the table name or its alias so that there is no ambiguity in the data requested

Example:

```
SELECT         stor_name, qty, t.title_id, title
FROM           titles  t
JOIN sales sal  ON    t.title_id = sal.title_id
JOIN stores st  ON    st.stor_id = sal.stor_id
```

Notice that we only have to use the alias on the title_id column where there is an ambiguity. You can get the required value title_id from either the titles table (which logical) or the sales table .Also, the join clause does not have to involve the data being selected it is merely there to access the tables

6A.5b Adding a filter (WHERE) when you use JOIN syntax

To illustrate a filter in the predicate logic, look at this code to see how a WHERE clause is added under each scenario

SQL Server Example: Return all store names whose name starts with B, the Quantity and the titles of the books sold

```
SELECT      stor_name, qty, title
FROM        titles t,  stores st,  sales sal
WHERE       t.title_id = sal.title_id
AND         st.stor_id = sal.stor_id
AND         stor_name  LIKE 'B%'
```

ANSI Example: Return all store names whose name starts with B, the Quantity and the titles of the books sold

```
SELECT      stor_name, qty, title
FROM        titles t
JOIN        sales sal      ON t.title_id = sal.title_id
JOIN        stores st      ON st.stor_id = sal.stor_id
WHERE       stor_name      LIKE 'B%'
```

The obvious question is "Which should I use, ANSI or SQL Server?"
The answer is that ANSI is more universal and it is up to you. You should be able to read both – it is not difficult

A join without restriction produces the Cartesian Product of the tables (see section 6A.2)

6A.6 Self joins (joins within one table)

Self joins correlate rows of a table with other rows of the same table
and joins by comparing a column with itself in the same table. The technique for doing this is to pretend that there are two tables by using two aliases

Aliasing
Because a self join involves only one table you have to assign aliases in order to create references that can logically refer to the two tables

The syntax is either:
   'alias' = table_name
   table_name alias (note the blank as a separator)

Example:
Return all titles which have the same price
```
SELECT     t1.title, t2.title, t1.price
FROM       titles t1, titles t2
WHERE      t1.price = t2.price
AND        t1.title_id < t2.title_id
```

Note: once you establish an alias you have to refer to that table ONLY by the alias (even in the select_list)

Self joins use the same set of operators as natural joins
   (except for OUTER JOIN operators)

The example will choose each row where the price is the same as another rows price within the same table (for each price)

Note: the < in the AND constraint ensures that you don't get the same entry in both columns or the other way round
(i.e. only one direction: a + b not both a + b & b + a)

ANSI syntax example:
Return all titles which have the same price
```
SELECT     t1.title, t2.title, t1.price
FROM       titles t1 JOIN titles t2
ON         t1.price = t2.price
AND        t1.title_id < t2.title_id
```

- Notice there is very little syntax difference between SQL Server syntax and the ANSI syntax. You can just substitute the word JOIN for the comma between the names of the tables and then use the word ON instead of the word WHERE.
- The ANSI syntax has an advantage of clarifying that the join is defined in the FROM section and not jumbled up in the filter (WHERE) section of your code

6A.7 Outer joins

An outer join allows you to restrict the rows in one table while not restricting the rows in the other i.e. you get all the rows in the column which forms the outer join and only the restricted rows in the other table

Example (ANSI syntax)
Return all the stores and lists the publishers if the publisher is in the same state as the store (otherwise a NULL)

SELECT	pub_name, stor_name, stores.state
FROM	publishers
RIGHT OUTER JOIN	stores
ON	publishers.state = stores.state

The resultset is returned as follows:

	pub_name	stor_name	state
1	NULL	Eric the Read Books	WA
2	Algodata Infosystems	Barnum's	CA
3	Algodata Infosystems	News & Brews	CA
4	NULL	Doc-U-Mat: Quality Laundry and Books	WA
5	Algodata Infosystems	Fricative Bookshop	CA
6	NULL	Bookbeat	OR

Rules:
1. Outer joins return **all** rows in the outer table
2. Can be used only between tables
3. You cannot use an IS NULL search conditions in the inner table

It is often useful to join a Foreign Key table to its Primary key table

Example: This lists all titles in the titles table and details of the sales
- if there are no sales - return NULL

SELECT	title, stor_id, ord_num, qty, ord_date
FROM	sales
LEFT OUTER JOIN	titles
ON	titles.title_id = sales.title_id

Old SQL Server syntax example:

```
SELECT    pub_name, stor_name, stores.state
FROM      publishers, stores
WHERE     publishers.state =* stores.state
```

If you try this in SQL Server 2008 onwards, you might get this or a similar message:

Msg 4147, Level 15, State 1, Line 3
The query uses non-ANSI outer join operators ("*=" or "=*"). To run this query without modification, please set the compatibility level for current database to 80, using the SET COMPATIBILITY_LEVEL option of ALTER DATABASE.
It is strongly recommended to rewrite the query using ANSI outer join operators
(LEFT OUTER JOIN, RIGHT OUTER JOIN). In the future versions of SQL Server, non-ANSI join operators will not be supported even in backward-compatibility modes.

6A.7a Using NULL in search conditions

For rows in the outer table that have no matching
rows in the inner table a NULL will be returned

You should not use NULL in the inner table search
conditions because you will get unexpected results

Example: (remember - this does NOT work)
Return all the sales of all the titles even if there are no sales

SELECT	title, stor_id, ord_num, qty, ord_date
FROM	sales s
RIGHT OUTER JOIN	titles t
ON	s.title_id = t.title_id
AND	qty IS NULL (qty is in the sales (INNER) table)

However, NULLS could be used in a column used for the OUTER JOIN
because a NULL will not be matched to the INNER table

6A.8   Theta join

Joins that use relational operators are called theta joins
They are based on a comparison of scalar values
by using =, > , >= , < , <= , < >, !<, !>

Example:

SELECT	title, stor_id,
	ord_num,
	qty,
	ord_date,
	pub_date
FROM	sales s
JOIN	titles t
ON	t.title_id = s.title_id
AND	pub_date > ord_date

6B SUBQUERIES

You can use a subquery in place of a value or an expression

Subqueries that have no dependancy on the outer query are called self-contained subqueries

This results in nesting of levels of queries/subqueries

However, there are some rules that apply because a subquery
only has a subset of SELECT statement functionality available to it

These nested 'inner' queries are termed Subqueries

A SELECT statement that uses subqueries can produce the same results as a join. Here is an example of such a use of a subquery:

Example:

```
SELECT      DISTINCT pub_name
FROM        publishers p
JOIN        titles t
ON          p.pub_id = t.pub_id
WHERE       type = "business"
```

returns the same results as:

```
SELECT      pub_name
FROM        publishers
WHERE       pub_id IN
            (SELECT     pub_id
             FROM       titles
             WHERE      type = "business")
```

Results of subqueries:

1. They can return zero or more values or serve as an existence checker

2. A subquery can return more than one row but only one column
Subqueries that return only one value are termed **scalar** subqueries while subqueries that return more than one value are termed **multi-valued**

3 When a single value is returned by the subquery it can
    be used whenever a single value can be used
        i.e. you can write your own functions
    If multiple values are returned when only 1 value was expected a
        NULL is returned

4 When a column is returned by the subquery it can be
    used anywhere an expression can be used

5 Columns from a table that appears **only** in the subquery
    cannot be included in the output
    (output is defined in the select_list of the outer query)

Note: Many subqueries can be formulated as joins
    There is no significant performance difference
        except where existence must be checked
        then a join will yield better performance
            because a subquery must be processed for each result in the outer query

Another example of a JOIN – SUBQUERY comparison

The diffirence between the queries is that 'state' cannot be included in the subquery because it is only included in the subquery. While the join query allows this.

Example using a Subquery
```
    SELECT   t.title_id, title, qty, price
    FROM     titles t
    JOIN     sales s ON t.title_id = s.title_id
    WHERE    stor_id IN (SELECT stor_id
    FROM     stores WHERE state = 'CA')
```

If you wanted to return 'state' the query has to be written as a join query, as follws:

Example using a JOIN
```
    SELECT   t.title_id, title, qty, price, state
    FROM     titles t
    JOIN     sales sal ON t.title_id = sal.title_id
    JOIN     stores st ON sal.stor_id = st.stor_id
    WHERE    state = 'CA'
```

Both of the above queries yield the following resultset (except the 'state')

	title_id	title	qty	price	state
1	PC8888	Secrets of Silicon Valley	50	20.00	CA
2	PS2091	Is Anger the Enemy?	75	10.95	CA
3	PS2091	Is Anger the Enemy?	10	10.95	CA
4	TC3218	Onions, Leeks, and Garlic: Cooking Secrets of t...	40	20.95	CA
5	TC4203	Fifty Years in Buckingham Palace Kitchens	20	11.95	CA
6	TC7777	Sushi, Anyone?	20	14.99	CA
7	BU7832	Straight Talk About Computers	15	19.99	CA
8	MC2222	Silicon Valley Gastronomic Treats	10	19.99	CA
9	BU2075	You Can Combat Computer Stress!	35	2.99	CA

6B.1 Nesting SELECT statements

Nesting can take place within the following statements:
   SELECT
   INSERT, UPDATE, DELETE (see next chapter for examples)

6B.2 Three types of subquery

1. With Comparison operators
2. Using the IN clause
3. Using the EXISTS clause

6B.2a with comparison operators

Example:
```
SELECT
   title_id,
   qty,
   Total = (SELECT sum(qty) FROM sales),
   % of Sales = (CONVERT(float,qty)/(SELECT sum(qty) FROM sales) )*100
FROM sales
```

Comparison operators can be modified by an ALL or ANY

A subquery introduced with an unmodified comparison
   operator MUST return only a single value
      i.e. you cannot use: >   <   !   NOT

The single result is then substituted in the outer query

6B.2b with the IN clause

The inner query (subquery) is evaluated first

The outer query then returns the rows that match the condition in the WHERE clause

The IN clause must be used instead of '=' if there are multiple values i.e. for a list of values

Example of IN without a subquery:

EX 1	SELECT	pub_name, city
	FROM	publishers
	WHERE	city IN ("boston", "washington")

Example of IN with a subquery:

EX 2	SELECT	pub_name, city
	FROM	publishers
	WHERE	pub_id IN
		(SELECT pub_id
		FROM titles
		WHERE type = "business")

Note: lists are returned in these circumstances even though an '=' is used

6B.2c with the EXISTS clause

A subquery returns TRUE or FALSE
   (Therefore it does not match 2 columns)

If the subquery returns TRUE then the row in the outer
   query is included in the result
If FALSE then it is not included

The subquery select_list is always * when used in an EXISTS clause

There is often no alternative to an EXISTS subquery

The keyword EXISTS is preceded only by WHERE

Example:

```
SELECT      pub_name
FROM        publishers
WHERE       EXISTS
            (
            SELECT      *
            FROM  titles
            WHERE       publishers.pub_id = titles.pub_id
            AND         type = "business"
            )
```

EXISTS also has a NOT EXISTS compliment

6B.3 Subquery restrictions/rules

1. A subquery can only use a subset of SELECT statement functionality

2. A subquery is always enclosed in parens

3. If the WHERE clause of the outer statement includes a column name it must be join compatible with the column name in the subquery select_list (i.e. it does not have to be a join but a join **must be possible** for the column to be selected)

4. If a subquery returns a single value it can be used wherever an expression is allowed (except in an ORDER BY clause)

5. Columns of text or image data cannot be used in a subquery

6. Subqueries introduced with a comparison operator cannot include GROUP BY or HAVING clauses

7. A subquery cannot include:
    ORDER BY
    COMPUTE
    the INTO keyword
    therefore they cannot manipulate results internally

Note: the DISTINCT keyword can effectively order the results because the system eliminates duplicates by ordering the results first
Subqueries maintain an implied DISTINCT within their execution because they will return the first instance encountered

8. The DISTINCT keyword cannot be used with subqueries that use the GROUP BY clause

9. The select_list of a subquery which is introduced with a comparison operator can include only one expression or column name

10 When a subquery is part of an equality expression
   the server will resolve the subquery first therefore
   the subquery must return only a single row
   (you have to use either:
   - *a unique identifier*
   - *an aggregate function)*

11 EXISTS operates on *

12 IN can operate on a select_list

6B.4 Correlated subqueries
(also known as *repeating subqueries*)

A Correlated subquery is one in which the WHERE clause in the subquery references a table in the FROM clause of the outer query

This means that the subquery is evaluated for each row selected by the outer query

Thus the name - 'repeating subquery' because the subquery is executed repeatedly, once for each row that is selected by the outer query
Therefore, the subquery depends on the outer query for its values.

Unlike most other subqueries a correlated subquery cannot be resolved independently of the main query

Example:

Return the title_id and royalty % for the author who enjoys the highest % royalty.

```
SELECT      title_id, au_id,
            royaltyper
FROM        titleauthor ta
WHERE       royaltyper =
            (
            SELECT      MAX(royaltyper)
            FROM        titleauthor
            WHERE       title_id = ta. title_id
            )
```

Note: the subquery is comparing the title_id column to the outer query's title_id column

Note2: the table only needs 1 alias to differentiate it from the direct reference (type it in - it works)

6C SELECT INTO statement

SELECT INTO creates a new table based on the
  results of a query
  using existing data definitions

The **new** table can be either temporary or permanent

A new permanent table can only be created if the
  'select into/bulk copy' option is set
  (use sp_helpdb to check if it is set)

Temporary tables are designated by using either # or ##
  ## means the temporary table is created as a global table

The inserted rows are not logged

If column headings are not set in the SELECT INTO statement
  then columns which are the result of an expression in
  the created table will not have column names.
  Therefore you should designate an alias as a column heading
  to prevent an error.

If set column headings should not contain spaces in the
  SELECT INTO statement
  but they can be aliased in subsequent queries

Example:

1	SELECT	Title = SUBSTRING(title,1,35),
		AvgMthlySales = ytd_sales/12
	INTO	#mthsalestable
	FROM	titles
2	SELECT	Title,
		"Avg Sales" = AvgMthlySales
	FROM	#mthsalestable

To select rows into a table that already exists INSERT must
  be used, not SELECT INTO - see next section

6D   UNION operator

UNION combines the result sets of any number of queries

Whereas a JOIN causes an increase in columns
> A UNION causes an increase in rows

Rules:
1. The column/expression structure has to match (number and order)
2. datatypes have to be compatible and are converted to the greatest precision type
3. Fixed length char and binary columns take the greater length
4. Variable length (or mixed) columns stay variable

Duplicate rows are removed by default
> the ALL option includes duplicate rows

Column names are taken from the first SELECT statement

If an ORDER BY clause is included it sorts the entire result set

ORDER BY and COMPUTE are only allowed at the end of
> the UNION statement (not within individual queries)

This means the whole resultset is ordered (or the COMPUTE totals are
> calculated for the complete query

GROUP BY and HAVING are allowed only within individual queries

The first query only can contain an INTO clause

Performance is usually improved if a query is broken
> into multiple SELECT statements and then UNIONED

Example:
What advances have been given to authors who have had no books sold but books have been sent to stores on consignment?

```
SELECT      title, stor_name, ord_date, qty
INTO        #temptable
FROM        titles, sales, stores
WHERE       titles.title_id = sales.title_id
AND         stores.stor_id = sales.stor_id

UNION
```

```
SELECT      title, "No Sales", null, null
FROM        titles
WHERE       title_id NOT IN (SELECT title_id FROM sales)

ORDER BY    qty desc
COMPUTE     sum(advance)
```

Note: the 1st set is derived from 3 joined tables and the
2nd set adds the titles that have no sales

Evaluation order is left to right unless controlled with parens

Example:
> X UNION ALL (Y UNION Z)

The UNION operator can also be used with an INSERT statement

Example:

```
SELECT      pub_id, pub_name, city
INTO        results
FROM        saleswest

UNION

SELECT      pub_id, pub_name, city
FROM        saleseast
```

The UNION operator can be useful when you want to modify some part of the result set but not all of it – you can then divide your query into two queries, treat them differently and then UNION them back together.

For example, if some prices are quoted per each and some per 100, you can use a UNION to divide the prices quoted per 100 by 100 – you just have to produce two result sets for each category and then concatenate the result back into one set with UNION

Chapter 7 – Modifying Data

Modifying Data

The whole point of maintaining a database is to be able to modify the data. Values are stored in columns which are part of instances of the entity (rows). Therefore modifications will be performed on rows. This part of SQL is known as DML (Data Manipulation Language)

There are three types of modification:
>
> INSERT
> UPDATE
> DELETE

While simple enough to say and understand, the conditions of applying them can be extremely complex

For example, whether an index is available for accessing the data and how effective is that index or whether the optimizer will choose it. These are topics covered elsewhere in this course and in subsequent courses on tuning SQL Server

They will play their part in scripting business processes. Much experience and judgement goes into planning and tuning which will take into consideration the set orientation of SQL Server processing

Cursors will be discussed in the chapter on programming SQL Server for row by row operations. Also set theory is the basis on which SQL Server performs and transactions will be dealt with later

It is not the intention to deal with these aspects at this stage, merely mentioning them here should suffice to alert the reader to the existence of other factors that affect the environment of data modification operations

The syntax of the T-SQL statements are examined here, but there are many other factors affecting the performance of operations

With this acknowledgment the subject is introduced

Chapter 7: Modifying Data

This module is designed to enable you to:

1. Add new rows with an INSERT statement
2. Insert, Update and Delete rows
3. Use data in other tables to determine which rows to update or delete
4. Use data in other tables as the data for updating
5. Update and remove rows based on information from other tables

Outline - The Context Tool

7A Inserting Rows 5

7A.1 The INSERT statement 5
       7A.1a DEFAULT keyword 7
       7A.1b INDENTITY keyword 7
       7A.1c Inserting Partial Data 8
7A.2 Inserting rows with SELECT 9
7A.3 INSERT EXEC 9
7A.4 INSERT INTO 9

7B Updating Row Data 10

7B.1 The UPDATE statement 10
7B.2 Update-in-place 11
7C.3 Updating based on data from other tables 13

7C Deleting Rows 14

7C.1 The DELETE statement 14
7C.2 Deleting based on data from other tables 15

7A INSERTING ROWS

T-SQL INSERT statements include:
1. INSERT . . . VALUES   one row of data
2. INSERT SELECT   multiple rows of data
3. INSERT EXEC   result of a sp or dynamic batch
4. SELECT INTO   a new table

7A.1 The INSERT statement

INSERT is used to add rows to a table (or View)
> it can be used with a VALUES keyword
> or with a SELECT statement

Syntax with VALUES keyword:
INSERT [INTO] table_name (column_list)
> **VALUES values_list/SELECT_Statement**

Example with VALUES keyword:
> Add a new author to the authors table

> > **INSERT authors**
> > **VALUES ('123 45 6789','Chisom','Dave','888 555 1212',**
> > **1234 Main Street','Thistown','CA','92000',0)**

Keywords:
> INSERT table_name (column_list)
> > the table_name can be a view_name
> > > (if only one table is included in the column list)
> >
> > the column_list is optional
> > the default column_list is the table columns in the
> > > order they occur in the table

> VALUES specifies the data to be inserted
> > it must be in the same order as the column list
> > variables can be provided in the values list

Note: SQL Server has to be able to fill the columns in a row with:
> - Data
> - defaults
> - NULLS
> that pass the constraint restrictions, etc

Chapter 7 - Modifying Data

Rules for inserting rows:

INSERT will only insert one row of data

Data values are inserted in the same order as the column names
    in the original CREATE TABLE statement

VALUES data is surrounded by parentheses
    and all character data is enclosed in single quotation marks

Use a separate INSERT statement for each row that you add

An empty string (' ') into a *varchar* or *text* column inserts a single space

All trailing spaces are removed from data inserted into *varchar* columns,
    except in strings that contain only spaces
    which are truncated to a single space

All fixed *'char'* columns are right-padded to the defined length

If an INSERT statement violates a constraint, default, or rule,
    or if it is the wrong datatype,
    the statement fails and SQL Server displays an error message

Inserting a null value into a *text* or *image* column
    does not create a valid text pointer,
    and does not preallocate a 2K text page

When you specify values for only some of the columns in the *column_list*,
    one of three things can happen to the columns that have no values:

1.   A default value is entered:
        - if the column has a DEFAULT constraint,
        - if a default is bound to the column,
        - if a default is bound to the underlying user-defined datatype.

2.   NULL is entered if the column allows NULLs and no default
        value exists for the column.

3.   An error message is displayed and the row is rejected
        if the column is defined as NOT NULL and no default exists

7A.1a Default options

Inserts the default values for all columns if there is no other value supplied by an INSERT

Syntax:
INSERT tablename DEFAULT VALUES

A DEFAULT value must be a constant, that is acharacter string, a scalar value (system or user-defined) or a NULL

If the column has either an IDENTITY property
    or If the column has a timestamp datatype
    then the next appropriate value will be inserted

If an identity column or timestamp is included in the column list then you have to specify ALL
    the columns in the column list
    except the Identity & Timestamp columns

If there is no specified default and NULL is allowed then NULL will be inserted

If the column has no specified default **and**
    does not allow NULL then
    an error will be returned and the INSERT statement rejected

DEFAULT

The use of DEFAULT in an INSERT statement specifies that
    the default value should be inserted in that column

Example:
VALUES (DEFAULT, expression, expression, DEFAULT, . . . etc

    i.e. The 'value' for the column default should not be
        specified in an INSERT statement only the word
        'DEFAULT' should be used

DEFAULT is not a valid value for an Identity column
    the value of an Identity or timestamp column should not be
    specified in an INSERT statement at all

In past and present version of SQL Server a DEFAULT can be created
    independently but this feature may be removed from T-SQL in the future so
    it would be best to not use it and just create defaults in Table definitions

Example of CREATE table with default column:
   The publishers table in the pubs database

```
CREATE TABLE [dbo].[publishers](
    [pub_id]      [char](4)       NOT NULL,
    [pub_name]    [varchar](40)   NULL,
    [city]        [varchar](20)   NULL,
    [state]       [char](2)       NULL,
    [country]     [varchar](30)   NULL
GO
ALTER TABLE [dbo].[publishers] ADD  DEFAULT ('USA') FOR
    [country]
```

7A.1b INDENTITY keyword

Although this section is not supposed to be about creating tables, an IDENTITY columnn is only created in the CREATE Table statement definition so in order to properly understand it we can look at the way an IDENTITY column is established

In a column definition the IDENTITY keyword indicates that a column is an IDENTITY column

When a new row is added to the table, the Database Engine provides a unique, incremental value for the column based upon a seed value and an increment

The IDENTITY property can be assigned to tinyint, smallint, int, bigint, decimal(p,0), or numeric(p,0) columns

Only one IDENTITY column can be created per table

DEFAULTs cannot be used with an identity column

Both the seed and increment or neither (seed or increment) must be specified. If neither is specified, the default is (1,1)

Identity columns are typically used with PRIMARY KEY constraints to serve as the unique row identifier for the table

You can reference it
   but you should omit it when not necessary to the statement

Example:
```
CREATE TABLE names
    (
    name_id      int    IDENTITY(1,1),
    fname        char(12)
    )

INSERT     table_name
VALUES     ("Cliff")
```

Notice that the name is inserted but not a value for the identity column. In fact the identity value is not even referred to – just omitted. Since the seed is 1 and the increment is 1, if the insertion was the 34th row then the identity column (name_id) would be a value of 34 – automagically calculated by SQL Server

Not shown in the example is that the name_id column would be defined as the Primary Key

7A.1c Inserting partial data

The INSERT statement can specify a column list

Any column that is not listed will be filled in with one of the following:

1	a specified DEFAULT value set for that column
2	timestamp datatype
3	be an IDENTITY column
4	allow NULLS

or an error will be displayed

The INSERT clause will use the above 4 alternatives where the column_list does not list the column

Therefore every column has to be covered by either the column_list or one of the four alternatives above

Example:
```
INSERT     publishers (pub_id, pub name)
VALUES     ('9975', 'Unbound Press')
```

If you run the statement

```
SELECT      *
FROM        publishers
WHERE       pub_name = 'Unbound Press'
```

You will get the report:

pub_id	pub_name	city	state	country
9975	Unbound Press	(null)	(null)	USA

illustrating NULLS and a default

Example: CREATE table for the publishers table in the pubs database

```
CREATE TABLE [dbo].[publishers](
    [pub_id]       [char](4)       NOT NULL,
    [pub_name]     [varchar](40)   NULL,
    [city]         [varchar](20)   NULL,
    [state]        [char](2)       NULL,
    [country]      [varchar](30)   NULL
GO
```

Also you can add a default like this:

ALTER TABLE [dbo].[publishers] ADD DEFAULT ('USA') FOR [country]

7A.2 INSERT SELECT (Inserting multiple rows)

Using SELECT allows the insertion of rows into a table from:
- *another table*
- *the same table*

Syntax using a SELECT statement:

INSERT	table_name
SELECT	column_list
FROM	table_list
WHERE	search_conditions

While the INSERT (with a VALUES keyword) statement inserts only one row the INSERT SELECT can insert many rows

Example:

Scenario: You want each author to sell books so you decide to set each author up as a store. You can do this by setting (in the stores table) a store for each author in the author's table using the last four digits of the author's Id for the store Id

```
INSERT    stores
SELECT    substring(au_id, 8, 4),
              au_lname,
              address,
              city,
              state,
              zip
FROM      authors
```

Rules:

The column_list and the result set of the SELECT statement must be compatible datatypes

If any column is omitted ensure a valid alternative is available (see section 1C above)

Note: So allow NULLS unless there is a good reason not to

Chapter 7 - Modifying Data

Syntax using a SELECT statement
	INSERT	table_name
	SELECT	column-list
	FROM	table_list
	WHERE	search_conditions

7A.3 INSERT EXEC

For an INSERT EXEC insert a stored procedure is used instead of a SELECT statement. Stored procedures are so powerful that you can do virtually anything, including passing parameters to them dynamically. So their advantage over a SELECT is that the WHERE filter conditions can be set dynamically

Example:
Scenario (same as above): You want each author to sell books so you decide
to set each author up as a store. You can do this by setting (in the stores table) a store for each author in the author's table using the last four digits of the author's Id for the store Id

```
INSERT      stores (
            substring(au_id, 8, 4),
            au_lname,
            address,
            city,
            state,
            zip
            )
EXEC        dbo.sproc_order_input
```

A major advantage of a Stored Procedure is that you can pass a parameter to a SP – see later Chapter on Stored Procedures

7A.4 INSERT .... INTO

The SELECT INTO statement copies data from a table or a view according to a SELECT and inserts it into a new table. So the SELECT ... INTO statement can be thought of as a combination of the SELECT and INSERT statements

The SELECT ... INTO statement is fast because a SELECT ... INTO transaction is not logged.

In order to use SELECT ... INTO to create a new permanent table, you have to explicitly turn on the database-option by running the sp_dboption stored procedure, as follows:

EXEC sp_dboptions pubs, 'select into/bulkcopy', True

The target table of this command can be either a regular permanent table or (is often) a temporary table:

A permanent table would not have a suffix in the name, like this

Example:
```
SELECT   au_fname, au_lname
INTO     authors_ca
FROM     authors
WHERE    state='CA'
```

A temporary table is designated by using a preffix in the name:

Example:
```
SELECT   au_fname, au_lname
INTO     #authors_ca
FROM     authors
WHERE    state='CA'
```

Notice the # as the first character of the table name – this denotes a temporary local table (local to the process). A double # sign (##) is used to create a temporary global table (global in tempdb) that can be accessed from other databases on the server

Chapter 7 - Modifying Data

Temporary tables come in different types including:

1. #   local temporary tables
2. ##   global temporary tables
3. prefixed by TempDB.. persistent temporary tables
4. @   table variables

Because temporary tables are never included in backup, you don't need to use the sp_dboption command before using SELECT . . . INTO with a temporary table

It is beyond our scope here to go into more detail on temporary table – simply know that they exist

7B   UPDATING ROW DATA

7B.1 The UPDATE statement

The UPDATE statement changes all data in existing rows in a table
   that matches the search conditions and provides the new data

UPDATE can only operate on one table

UPDATE statements consist of 3 main components

1   The **table** to be updated

2   The **columns** to be updated
        SET is a required keyword that specifies
            the columns and the changed values
            columns are specified as
                a column_list
                    SET column_name = {expression | NULL}
                a variable_list
                    SET variable_name = {expression | NULL}

   Remember from Chapter 3 that an expression can be a
   a column_name, a variable, a constant, a function, and
       any combination of the above connected by an operator,
       or a subquery (but aggregates are not allowed)

3   The **rows** to be updated (in the WHERE clause)

   searched UPDATE {search_conditions}
       specify the criteria for a searched update

   positioned UPDATE {CURRENT OF cursor_name}
       specifies only the single current row of the specified cursor

   If there is no WHERE clause - every row in the table is updated

Syntax:

```
UPDATE      table_name
SET             {table_name | view_name}
                {column_list | variable_list | variable and column list} = expression
WHERE       search_conditions | CURRENT OF cursor_name}
```

Chapter 7 - Modifying Data

Example 1: If a user had been eroneously entering California as CN and Oakland as Owklan (you just can't get decent help these days) you might want to run the following:

```
UPDATE      authors
SET         state = 'CA', city = 'Oakland'
WHERE       state = 'CN' AND city = 'Owklan'
```

Example of a single row update: alter the price of a book

```
UPDATE      titles
SET         price = $5.99
WHERE       title_id = 'BU2075'
```

More Examples:

1. Raise the discount 10% for quantities over 100
   ```
   UPDATE discounts
       SET         discount = discount * 1.1
       WHERE       lowqty >= 100
   ```

2. Searched UPDATE
   Change the name of a publisher
   ```
   UPDATE publishers
       SET         pub_name = "Cliff's Press'
       WHERE       pub_id = '1234'
   ```

   If you used only
   ```
   UPDATE      publishers
   SET         pub_name = "Cliff's Press'
   ```
   this would set every row in the publisher table to 'Cliff's Press' because there is no WHERE clause restriction

3. Positioned UPDATE
   Change the name of a publisher in a cursor
   ```
   UPDATE      publishers
   SET         pub_name = "Cliff's Press'
   WHERE CURRENT OF pub_id = '1234'
   ```
   this updates the row that the cursor is active on

If integrity constraints are violated the entire UPDATE is rolled back.
IDENTITY columns should not be updated

Chapter 7 - Modifying Data

7B.2 Updating based on data from other tables

A table can be updated using data from other tables

A FROM clause lists the data sources

Each row in the target table has to meet the criteria in the
    outer WHERE clause

A single UPDATE statement never updates the same row twice
    therefore it may be necessary to use a nested SELECT
    statement to aggregate the data

Example:

Replace the ytd_sales qty with the aggregate sum(qty) from the sales table

```
UPDATE   titles
SET   ytd_sales =   (SELECT    sum(qty)
                     FROM      sales
                     WHERE     sales.title_id = titles.title_id
                     AND       ord_date BETWEEN '01/01/95'
                                        AND '12/31/95')
FROM     titles, sales
```

Note: For each row in the target table the nested SELECT
    statement must only be executed once
    If it returns >1 value the results are unpredictable

Table joins provide exclusive search criteria for the WHERE clause

There can be an OUTER WHERE clause and an INNER WHERE clause

The Outer WHERE clause (in the main statement) determines
    the rows to be updated

The Inner WHERE clause (in a nested SELECT) determines
    the data to be used in the update process

Note:
    A transaction is always implied with the UPDATE statement

Chapter 7 - Modifying Data

7C   DELETING ROWS

7C.1 The DELETE statement

DELETE removes one or more rows from a table as specified in the WHERE clause

Only entire rows can be deleted with the DELETE statement

Note: You cannot delete a column

Syntax:

DELETE [FROM]   table_name
WHERE   {*search_conditions* | CURRENT OF *cursor_name*}

If no WHERE clause is specified then ALL records will be deleted
The word FROM is optional so is usually not used

Example 1:   **Remove all sales records more than 3 or more years old**

DELETE   sales
WHERE   DATEDIFF(YEAR, ord_date, GETDATE()) >= 3

Example 2: to delete all the rows in the authors table

DELETE   authors

This does not act in the same way as TRUNCATE
While the DELETE statement without a WHERE clause is
    functionally equivalent to the TRUNCATE TABLE statement
    the TRUNCATE statement is faster because DELETE logs
    all the row deletions

Example 2:   **DELETE a Set of Rows**
Because *au_fname* may not be unique, this example deletes all rows where *au_fname* is Anne

DELETE FROM   authors
WHERE   au_fname = 'Anne'

Example 3: DELETE the Current Row of a Cursor
This illustates a delete made against a cursor
and deletes the selected row (the row that has been fetched)

DELETE FROM   authors
WHERE CURRENT OF cursor_name

7C.2 Removing rows based on data from other tables

The WHERE clause can access other tables by using a FROM clause
This is functionally similar to a correlated subquery

Syntax:
DELETE [FROM] table_name
FROM table_name
WHERE clause

Example:
Delete all rows in the titleauthor table where the title contains the word 'computers'

1 Subquery

```
DELETE      titleauthor
WHERE       au_id IN
            (SELECT a.au_id
            FROM   authors a
            JOIN   titles t
                   ON a.au_id = ta.au_id
            JOIN   titleauthur ta
                   ON titleauthor.title_id = t.title_id
            WHERE  t.title LIKE '%computers%)
```

This query deletes the row in titleauthor that is selected by
the subquery defined by the 2 joins that connect the 3 tables
1   WHERE titleauthor.title_id = t.title_id
2   AND a.au_id = ta.au_id

2 T-SQL Extension

DELETE	[FROM] titleauthor	--*a 'Delete it' FROM*
FROM	authors a , titles t	--*a 'Select it' FROM*
WHERE	a.au_id = ta.au_id	
AND	titleauthor.title_id = t.title_id	
AND	t.title LIKE '%computers%'	

This query deletes the row in titleauthor that is defined by
    a WHERE clause standard option

DELETE with no parameters will delete all rows from the table

Author's note: The second FROM is optional

When creating DELETE ststement you should:

    1   write a SELECT statement
    2   test that it returns the desired results
    3   then create the DELETE

CHAPTER 8:

VIEWS

Should a user be able to see all of a table if they have permission to access that table?

Should a user have to deal with joins, isn't there another way?

Can we physically store data in one way and access it in logical groupings so that the complexity is hidden from the user?

SQL Server provides an alternative method of accessing the data - a view

This may be thought of as the creation of virtual tables.

By definition virtual tables do not exist physically
    but in most cases they may be treated as if they do

Basically a view is a predefined resultset
    This has advantages and disadvantages
    They can be used in joins
    They add to the complexity of the database.
    They can be used to update the database.
    They have limitations, rules and options.

We will look at these in this chapter.

Chapter 8:

Views

Outline - The Context Tool

8	**Views**	5
8A	What is a view?	5
8B	Considerations	
	1B.1 Advantages of views	6
	1B.2 Some characteristics of views	6
8C	Creating and dropping views	8
8D	View information	9
8E	View options	
	1E.1 WITH CHECK option	10
	1E.2 WITH ENCRYPTIONS option	10
8F	Projection example	11
8G	Join example	12
8H	A view of a view example	12
8I	Computed column example	13
8J	Aggregate functions example	13
8K	Modifying data through views	14
8L	Modifications affecting tables with NOT NULL columns	14
8M	Views as security mechanisms	15

Chapter 8 - Views

8A What is a View?

A view is an alternate way of looking at data in a database
(contrasting to selecting all the columns in a particular table
and are often used to define a frequently accessed record which
involves joined tables

It consists of selected columns from 1 or more tables (or other views)
often called base tables

In addition to selected columns, views allow calculated or derived columns

A view does not consist of any data, a stored query of that data,
so creating a view has no effect on underlying tables only a read-only
SELECT statement

To look at the available views - from SSMS - Choose
ObjectExplorer>>Databases>>DatabaseName>>Views from the tree
list of objects

RtClick on a view, select Script View as >> CREATE TO >> New Query
Editor Window and SSMS will display it in a new editor pane

If a base table is dropped using the view will result in a error message
but when the base table become available again the view will also be
usable

8B Advantages of views:

1. **Focus**: allows users to focus on only the data in which they are interested
2. **Reusability**: creating a view for frequently used queries enables reuse without having to recreate the query (write once, use it forever)
3. **Customization**
4. **Security**: enables allocation of security to different users

For example, you might define a view that joins the *titles*, *authors*, and *titleauthor* tables to display the names of the authors and the books they have written. This view would hide personal data about authors and financial information about the books

The WITH CHECK OPTION set in the create view statement forces all data modification statements executed against that view to adhere to the criteria set within the SELECT statement defining the view

To provide security a user's (or group's) access may be restricted to:
- *a subset of rows*
- *a subset of columns*
- *a row and column subset*
- *rows that qualify for a join between >1 table*
- *a subset of another view*
- *a statistical summary*

Data from a view can be exported to another application using the bcp (bulk copy program) utility

8B.1   View considerations

Objects referenced in a view are verified during creation

Dropping underlying objects (tables) does not drop the view
      but there will be an error message next time the view is used

If you define a view using a SELECT * and then add columns
      the new columns do not appear in the view. This is because
      the * is interpreted and expanded only when the view is created

Views have a hidden complexity (caused by depth of levels)
      which may be hard to track

This is particularly important when assessing the number of joins in a
      query. A Naming-standard should indicate that it is a view
      or the number of a query's underlying joins can cause a surprise

It is recommended that views are named with an identifying prefix
      to differentiate them from tables

          For example: vwMyView

8C Creating Views

Example of a view

Table 1 - Table

Name	id	Rank	M/F	No	unit
Gail	12A	Capt	F	2	12
Anne	32H	Pvt	F	3	20
Joe	62D	Pvt	M	1	10

View 1

Rank	Name	No	unit
Capt	Gail	2	12
Pvt	Anne	3	20
Pvt	Joe	1	10

Syntax:

CREATE VIEW view_name [col_name, col_name, etc]
AS select_statement
[WITH CHECK OPTION]

When creating a view you should:

1. write the SELECT statement
2. test that it returns the desired results
3. then create the view

Creating a view does not display it
   You have to write a separate SELECT statement

If column names are omitted from the view statement the
   view columns inherit the table column names

You can name column names in the AS SELECT statement

Example:

Step 1   **CREATE VIEW author_names**
AS
SELECT
    FirstName = authors.au_fname
    LastName = authors.au_lname
FROM
    authors

Step 2   **SELECT   ***
             FROM   author_names

Rules:

You must have permission to SELECT the underlying objects (including tables) in a view when using a view

Temporary tables cannot be used in views therefore SELECT INTO cannot be used

Outer joins can return unpredictable results
    All rows in the inner table are returned
    Rows in the outer table may return a NULL for rows that do
        not meet the qualification criteria

You cannot create a default, a trigger or an index on a view

CREATE VIEW statements cannot be combined with other SQL statements

The UNION operator cannot be used within a CREATE VIEW statement

Views can contain:
- Aggregate functions and grouping
- Joins
- Other views
- A DISTINCT clause

Views cannot contain:
- SELECT INTO
- An ORDER BY clause

8C.1 Dropping Views

Syntax:
DROP VIEW view_name

When you use DROP VIEW the definition and other information is dropped from the system tables

8D View information

When a view is created the following system tables are updated:

Sys Table	Stores
sysobjects	View names
sysprocedures	View normalized query tree
syscolumns	Columns defined in a view
sysdepends	View dependencies (also use for a trigger, stored procedure or table)
syscomments	Text of view creation statement

Use **sp_helptext** to view the text used to create a view (except when the ENCRYPTION option prevents it)

8E View options

8E.1 "WITH CHECK" option

Data modification statements on views do not check to ensure that data will remain within the original definition of the view

e.g. An INSERT can be issued on a view to add a row to a base table even if that row is not defined by the view
OR
An UPDATE can be issued that changes a row so that the row no longer meets the definition of the view

The "WITH CHECK OPTION" forces all data modification statements executed against a view to be checked against the original SELECT statement which defined the view

When a row is modified through a view the "WITH CHECK OPTION" guarantees that the data will remain visible through the view after modification

Response to the "WITH CHECK OPTION"

	Response	
	Option Not set	Option Set
IN range		
Insert/Update/Delete	Successful	Successful
Out of range		
Insert	Successful	Error
Update	(0 rows affected)	(0 rows affected)
Delete	(0 rows affected)	(0 rows affected)
IN range but value is Out of range	Successful	Error

8E.2 "WITH ENCRYPTION" option

This option encrypts the syscomments entries

After Encryption the view definition is no longer available

To Unencrypt you must drop and recreate the view

    Always use encryption rather than deleting entries in syscomments

8F Projection example

A projection is a sub-set of columns

Used when you want to see only specified columns

Example:

View definition:
```
CREATE VIEW   book_description
AS
SELECT        title, synopsis
FROM          title
```

Select:
```
SELECT        *
FROM          book_description
```

This example selects a subset consisting of:

columns:	only the title and sysnopsis columns
rows:	all the rows
from	the titles table

8G Join example

A join links the rows in 2 or more tables
    by comparing the values in a specified column

Used when you want to include columns from >1 table

Syntax: View definition:

```
CREATE VIEW vw_author_title_publisher
AS SELECT
    author.fname,
    author.lname,
    title.title,
    publisher.pub_name
FROM
    author, titleauthor, title, publisher
WHERE
    author.au_id = titleauthor.au_id
AND
    titleauthor.title_id = title.title_id
AND
    titles.pub_id = publisher.pub_id
```

Select:
```
SELECT      *
FROM        author_title_publisher
```

This example selects a subset consisting of columns from
    different tables utilizing joins to restrict the result set
    to relevant data only

Using a view benefits the user since it will be reusable
    without the user having to write the join statements in a query

Select:
```
SELECT DISTINCT    title, pub_name
FROM               author_title_publisher
```

Note: the use of the DISTINCT option to eliminate duplicates
    in the titles column

8H A view of a view example

Example:

```
CREATE VIEW  Total_Sales_Per_BusinessBook
AS SELECT    *
FROM         Total_Sales_Per_TypeOfBook
WHERE        type = "business"


SELECT       *
FROM         Total_Sales_Per_BusinessBook
```

Notice: that the example uses the previous view but because it has already been calculated the Total_Sale$ does not have to be recalculated. Thus, the user can interrogate the view without having to write the code to calculate the Total_Sales$

8I Computed column example

Example:

```
CREATE VIEW Total_Sales_Per_Title(Title, Qty_YTD_sales, Price, Total $)
    AS SELECT
        title,
        ytd_sales,
        price,
        (ytd_sales * price)
    FROM  titles

SELECT  *
FROM    Total_Sales_Per_Title
```

Note: The alternate way to name the columns in a view is to name them in the CREATE VIEW clause column name parameters

Views enable queries to be written which are specific to the user's needs

Columns that are computed cannot be modified through a view (or otherwise)

8J Aggregate functions example

Views can use aggregate functions

Example:

```
CREATE VIEW Total_Sales_Per_TypeOfBook
AS
SELECT
            type,
            Total_Sales$ = SUM(ytd_sales * price)
FROM        titles
GROUP BY    type

SELECT      *
FROM        Total_Sales_Per_TypeOfBook
```

Columns that are derived from aggregate functions cannot be modified through a view

8K Modifying data through views

While data can be modified by using a view, only one table can be modified

This limits the functionality of INSERT, UPDATE and DELETE

DELETE
You cannot DELETE rows from a view that uses >1 table

INSERT
INSERTS are not allowed into views except if all columns in the underlying tables which are not included in the view allow NULLs or have a defined default

stated another way
INSERTS are allowed on views that involve joins as long as:
1 the inserted columns belong to only one base table
2 all columns in the base table that:
   - do not allow NULLS and
   - have no defaults
   are included in the INSERT statement

UPDATE
UPDATE columns for >1 table require separate treatment

Example:
/* This is NOT permitted */
UPDATE titles_and_authors
SET type = "mod_cook", au_fname = "Mary"
WHERE title = "The Gourmet Microwave"

/* Do this instead */
UPDATE titles_and_authors
SET type = "mod_cook"
WHERE title = "The Gourmet Microwave"
GO
UPDATE titles_and_authors
SET au_fname = "Mary"
WHERE title = "The Gourmet Microwave"

Views containing a DISTINCT clause cannot be modified

8L Modifications to tables with NOT NULL columns

Modifications cannot be made to columns with:

- *computed values*
- *built in functions*
- *Row aggregate functions*

8M Views as security mechanisms

By defining different views and selectively granting permissions on them,
> a user (or any combination of users) can be restricted to different subsets of data

Through a view, users can query and modify only the data they can see

The rest of the database is neither visible nor accessible

Permission to access the subset of data in a view must be granted or revoked, regardless of the set of permissions in force on the view's underlying tables

When a users who has no access to data enters
> SELECT * FROM *table_name*

SQL Server expands the asterisk into a list of all the columns in the table
> and, since permission on some of these columns has been revoked for that user, refuses access to them and the user sees a "permission denied" message

So if CREATE VIEW permission has been granted and a view created, the user can access that data even if permission to the underlying table has been revoked

This hold true as long as the user holds SELECT permission of the view

The error message lists the columns for which the user is denied access.
To see all the columns for which they do have permission, users have to name the columns specifically

Context-sensitive permission
Views can also be used for context-sensitive permission

Example:
>A view can give a data-entry clerk permission to access only those rows that he or she has added or updated

Method:
1. Add a *user_-name* column to a table in which the login ID of the user entering each row will be automatically recorded with a default

2. Define a view that includes all the rows of the table where *user_name* is the current user, which can be checked with the SUSER_NAME() function
   E.G.
   >WHERE user_name = SUSER_NAME()

   The rows retrievable through the view now depend on the identity of the person who executes the SELECT statement against the view

Chapter 9 - Data Integrity

Businesses tend to establish organizational standard operating procedures that requiring certain policies (rules) be followed to ensure the business runs as planned. This can be thought of as *Business* Integrity.

Data Integrity merely refers to the accuracy and reliability of the data in a database and, like business integrity, also entails ensuring that certain rules are followed. Data must be correct and consistent throughout the database (e.g. not corrupt, orphaned/widowed or 'out of sync'). When planning the database and its tables it is important to think of how integrity is to be implemented.

Data may be thought of as consisting of collections of objects with various attributes and relationships. The ERA model defines an entity as a table, which is a collection of instances (Rows). Each instance has attributes (values in Columns). The relationships/connections are represented by matching values in columns (attributes) between tables. When a relationship/connection has been established it forms a result, which is the combination of the rows in the individual tables. This record will represent the data before normalization. These are the elements upon we must work to ensure data integrity.

Entity Integrity (table integrity) is enforced by ensuring that rows are unique for a particular table.

Although this is usually accomplished by enforcing the primary key of a table, it can also be enforced by using an IDENTITY column (attribute), unique indexes or unique constraint.

Domain Integrity (column integrity)

Columns (attributes) have defined domains. Values set the choice within the domain (set of possible values)
    e.g.   Green is the value of the Color attribute
              Bold is the value of the Type Style attribute

Therefore domain integrity is enforced by ensuring that values for a given column are valid in terms of a set of rules. It is enforced by restricting:
- the type (through datatypes),
- the format (through CHECK constraints and rules), or
- the range of possible values (through REFERENCES and CHECK constraints, defaults and rules).

Referential Integrity (RI)

Referential integrity is the process of preserving defined relationships between tables when you enter or delete records in those tables. Keeping data modifications consistent throughout a database enforces referential integrity. This means that the integrity of cross-table references is maintained (by using constraints). It involves managing corresponding data values between tables when the foreign key of a table (child table) contains the same values as the primary key of another table (parent table). Note: This is often erroneously envisioned the other way round).

There is some confusion regarding the definition of a parent and a child but think of it this way: A parent can exist without a child but every child has to have a parent.

Customer/Invoice example:

Every invoice has to have a customer (parent) while you can have customers who have no invoices. So the Invoice table is the child table and the Customers table is the parent table. The CustomerID is the Primary key and is thought of as the parent table. The Invoice table has a Foreign key (relating to the Primary key of the Parent) and is the child. However, intuition might cause you to think the other way round so it is a bit counter-intuitive. Some books omit defining the Parent/Child relationship and refer to the referencing table and the referenced table instead

The point here is that every column that has been defined as a Foreign key must have a Primary key in another table (every child has to have a parent). P for Primary, P for Parent

The Parent/Child analogy can confuse so maybe we should refer to it as the Primary-Key table and the Foreign-Key table

Chapter 9:

D A T A   I N T E G R I T Y

Outline - The Context Tool

9A	**Data Integrity**	5
9A.1	What is Data Integrity	5
9A.2	Four Types of Data Integrity	6
9A.3	Enforcing Data Integrity	8
9B	**Indentity property**	9
9B.1	Using IDENTITY columns	10
9C	**Defaults and Rules**	11
3C.1	Using Defaults to Enforce Data Integrity	12
3C.2	Using Rules to Enforce Data Integrity	13
3C.3	Binding Defaults and Rules	13
3C.4	Unbinding and Dropping Defaults and Rules	14
9D	**Constraints**	15
9D.1	Defining Constraints	16
9D.2	Implementing Constraints	17
9D.3	Types of Constraints	18
	9D.3a.1 Unique Constraints	18
	9D.3a.2 Primary Key Constraints	19
	9D.3b.1 Check Constraints	20
	9D.3b.2 Default Constraint	22
	9D.3c Foreign Key Constraints	24
9D.4	When to use Data Integrity Constraints	26
9D.5	Examples of CREATE TABLE statements	28

9A   Data Integrity

9A.1   What is Data Integrity?

Data Integrity refers to consistency and correctness of data in a database
this can be achieved by:
- validating the contents of individual columns
- verifying column values with one another
- validating data in one table against criteria in another
- verifying that the database has been successfully updated
         for each transaction

Non-relational database systems require data integrity logic
         to be *coded* into each application

SQL Server stores much of this logic in the database itself
         Rules in the application are, therefore, not needed
         Rules in the DBMS only have to be changed in one place.

Former options for SQL Server data integrity were restricted to
         defaults, triggers and rules
Data integrity enhancements can (in addition) now be implemented by
         the IDENTITY column/attribute/property and CONSTRAINTS

IDENTITY COLUMN generates values that uniquely identify a row and are
         implemented in the CREATE table statement

CONSTRAINTS are implemented by extending the data definition in
         ALTER table and CREATE table statements
These statements allow constraints to be placed on:
         -     individual columns (column level) or
         -     combinations of columns (table level)

With these two enhancements SQL Server offers
> two methods of defining data integrity logic on data:
>> 1   create one global object and apply (bind) it to various parts of data in the table
>> 2   create and apply at the creation level which means it is built in "one less step"

Declarative Referential Integrity (DRI) allows setting of data restrictions:
> 1   for a table
> 2   between tables (during INSERT, UPDATE & DELETE)

9A.2　Four Types of Data Integrity

	Type	Quick & Dirty Description
1	Entity Integrity	Row
2	Domain Integrity	Column
3	Referential Integrity	Links?
4	User defined Integrity	

9A.2a Entity Integrity (Row restrictions)

Requires all ROWS in a table to have a unique identifier
> • *the primary key value*

this results in a row being a unique entity within a table

The level of referential integrity between the primary key and any foreign keys determines:
> 1   whether the primary key value can be changed or
> 2   whether the row can be deleted

Enforced by
> • *UNIQUE constraints*
> • *PRIMARY KEY constraints*
> • *NULL constraint*
> • *UNIQUE indexes*
> • *IDENTITY datatype*

9A.2b Domain Integrity (Column restrictions)

Refers to the range (domain) of valid entries for a column

Defines:
- the set of data values that are valid
- whether NULL is allowed

Is enforced through:
- *restricting the data type*
  - system datatypes and user-defined datatypes
- *format*
  - Rules
  - CHECK constraints

- *range (of possible values)*
  - Rules
    - FOREIGN KEY constraints
    - CHECK constraints
    - NULL constraint
    - Default values
- *Triggers*
- *Stored procedures*

9A.3c Referential Integrity (restrictions based on columns in other tables)

ensures the relationship between:
- the primary keys (in the referenced table)
- the foreign keys (in the referencing table)

are always maintained

Child Table   **Parent Table**
                                   PK   x x x x x
FK   y y y y y ⟶
The   The
Referenc**ing**   Referenc**ed**
Table   Table

A row in the referenced table cannot be deleted
  if a foreign key references that row
  because this would create an 'Orphan'

A foreign key value cannot be inserted into the referencing table
  if no row exists in the referenced table
  because this would also create an 'Orphan'

Enforced through:

- *FOREIGN KEY constraint*
- *Triggers*
- *Stored procedures*

9A.4d User defined

Includes business rules that do not fall into the other categories

Enforced through:

- *FOREIGN KEY constraint*
- *CHECK constraint*
- *Rules*
- *Triggers*
- *Stored procedures*

9A.3   Enforcing Data Integrity

Integrity may be enforced either by:
- *1* Procedural methods
- *2* Declarative methods

9C.1   Procedural Data Integrity

is implemented using the DDL (Data Definition Language)
combined with the T-SQL language on the server

Implemented through Triggers which are automatically fired
and can call stored procedures (see Chapter 11)

Stored procedures need to be used in conjunction with
a trigger to achieve data integrity (see Chapter 12)

9C.2   Declarative Data Integrity

Advatages of using declarative integrity include:

is part of the database definition

is concise

is less error prone than procedural methods

is performed by the DBMS and not a developer

are defined directly on the tables and columns using
CREATE TABLE and ALTER TABLE

is enforced through:
constraints that restrict the data values that can be INSERTED
or UPDATED
and the IDENTITY property

The disadvantage of constraints is the lack of custom error
handling capabilities
(error handling has to be done by @@ERROR)

9B IDENTITY property/attribute

Is an automatically generated value
    based on the previous identity value
    to identify each row in a table

increments are specified in the table definition

can be placed on any one column in any order
    it is not a column in itself but the attribute/property of a column

the column has a name (like any other column)
    but values are not usually INSERTed by the user

Rules:
- only one column per table
- cannot be 'updated'
- NULLS are not allowed
- must be integer, or numeric or decimal with scale = 0

Syntax:

    IDENTITY (seed, increment)

Example:

```
CREATE TABLE class
    (
    student_id  int IDENTITY(100,5)
    name VARCHAR(16)
    )
INSERT   class
VALUES ('Steven")
```

The student_id column is created as an Integer with a starting value of 100 incremented by 5 each row

The result of **SELECT * FROM class** will be (say):

Student_id	Name
100	Steven

Chapter 9 – Data Integrity

9B.1 Using IDENTITY columns

IDENTITYCOL is a keyword used to reference an identity column

i.e. It is not necessary to remember the column name

Example:

SELECT * FROM class WHERE IDENTITYCOL = 150

@@IDENTITY returns the last value used

This may return:
190
(1 row affected)

The IDENTITY column should not be referenced if you are letting
it default to what SQL Server will insert

The *identity_insert* option:

    turns off the automatic generation and relies
        on the user to insert values in the IDENTITY column
        Note: IDENTITY does not enforce uniqueness
        (you have to use a UNIQUE index)

    the option is mostly used to insert a previously deleted row
    can be set only by the table owner, dbo or sa
    while *identity_insert* can be set on for one table at a time
        multiple users can use it at the same time

Example:
> **SET identity_insert Pubs . . class ON**

This sets the *identity_insert* property on for the table named class
(the table 'class' is not in the standard Pubs DB)

after the option has been set you can reference the IDENTITY column

Example 2:

Used to INSERT a previously deleted row

INSERT class (student_id, name)
VALUES (100, "Thomas")

Note: you must supply the column list in the INSERT statement

9C Creating and Implementing Defaults and Rules

Defaults and Rules are a valid method of enforcing Data Integrity
(but Constraints are preferred)

Defaults and Rules create objects that can be **bound** to a column
or a user defined data type

9C.1 DEFAULTS

Defaults specify a value to be inserted in a column to which
an object is bound

Syntax:
CREATE DEFAULT [owner.] default_name
AS constant_expression

Example:
CREATE DEFAULT def_ssn
AS '000-00-0000'

sp_bindefault def_ssn, ssn, FUTUREONLY

Note:

IF you do not specify NOT NULLS (no NULLS allowed)
AND no default is specified
THEN an error will occur whenever a user fails to enter
a value in the column
NULL is allowed as a default

Use a *default* instead of a *constraint* if it will be reused multiple columns

Defaults are checked only on INSERT

A default's scope is database wide so default names must be unique within a database

9C.2 RULES

Rules specify the acceptable values that can be inserted into a column

Syntax:
CREATE RULE [owner.] rule_name
AS condition_expression

Example:
CREATE RULE state_code_rule
AS @statecode in ('AZ', 'CA', 'PA')

Rules are checked on both INSERT and UPDATE
    but not against existing data when the rule is bound

A rule's scope is database wide so rule names must be unique within a database

Rules are bound with sp_bindrule to:
- a column
- a number of columns
- all columns in a database of a particular datatype

9C.1 Using Defaults to Enforce Data Integrity

A default needs to be the same datatype as the column

A default must adhere to the applicable rules and CHECK constraints

The column must be large enough for the default

The default on a column that allows NULLS and has no specified default is NULL

If you specify NOT NULL for a column then whether you
    enter NULL or make no entry you will get an error

9C.2 Using Rules to Enforce Data Integrity

Rules ensure that data INSERTed or UPDATEd:
- *falls within specified ranges of values*
- *matches certain patterns*
- *matches entries in a list*

Note: Rules are due to be removed from future versions of SQL Server so use Check Constraints where you can

Rules are CREATEd first and then bound to a column in a table

They must be compatible with the column or datatype they are bound to

A column or user defined datatype can only have one rule bound to it
When you bind a rule it will replace any existing rule on that column

This rule is checked each time a user enters a value

Rule definition can contain any expression that is valid in a
WHERE clause including:
- *arithmetic operators*
- *comparison operators*
- *LIKE*
- *IN*
- *BETWEEN*

however it cannot reference any column directly - nor any other database object

The AS clause

The parameter name is prefixed with an @ sign

Reads like a WHERE clause
Syntax example:
CREATE RULE fine_paid
AS @it = 20
OR @it < 7

Note: a parameter name can be specified more than once
typically the rule has the same name as the column to which it is bound

Rules have to be compatible with the column to which they are bound

9C.3 Binding Defaults and Rules

The process is:
> create the Default or Rule
> then
> bind the Default or Rule

use the sp_bindefault or sp_bindrule system stored procedure

Syntax:
> **sp_bindefault defname, objname, futureonly]**

Example:
> **sp_bindefault ss_no_default, SocSecNumber**

This example binds the default called ss_no_default to the user-defined datatype called SocSecNumber

Syntax:
> **sp_bindrule rulename, objname [,futureonly]**

Example:
> **sp_bindrule state_code_rule, 'members.statecode'**

> This example binds the rule called state_code_rule to the statecode column in the members table

futureonly is an optional parameter which prevents existing user defined datatypes (not column names) from inheriting any newly bound rules or defaults

You cannot bind a default or a rule to:
- a system datatype or
- a timestamp column

When there is a default or rule bound to both a user-defined datatype and a column, the column takes precedence

9C.2   Unbinding and Dropping Defaults and Rules

Unbinding a default or a rule detaches it from the
    user-defined datatype or column
but it still remains in the database until it is dropped with
    DROP DEFAULT or DROP RULE

You can, however, DROP a user-defined datatype (or a table)
    without unbinding a default

Syntax:
    sp_unbindefault defaultname, objname [,futureonly]

    sp_unbindrule rulename, objname [,futureonly]

Examples:
    sp_unbindefault ss_no_default, 'SocSecNumber'

    sp_unbindrule state_code_rule, 'members.statecode'

A new 'binding' automatically unbinds the old default or rule

If the object name is not in the form *table.column* SQLServer
    assumes it is a user-defined datatype

Dropping Defaults and Rules

NULLS allowed - SQLServer will insert NULL
NOT NULLS columns - error message if rows are added but with no
    entry in that column

Syntax:
    DROP DEFAULT [owner.] default_name

    DROP RULE [owner.] rule_name

Examples:
    DROP DEFAULT stop

    DROP RULE state_code_rule

The DROP command removes the default or rule from the database

Note: Run sp_help against the Pubs database
    There are 4 user defined types
        empid
        id

     ssn_type
     tid
    none of which have defaults or rules
There are 9 other defaults for columns
Only the owner can drop a default or rule

Defaults and Rules must be unbound before they can be dropped
but you can drop a user-defined datatype (or a table) without unbinding a default

9D Using Constraints to Enforce Data Integrity

Constraints may be looked on as rules that SQL Server enforces
> for you, restricting the *domain* of possible values that can be entered in a column (or columns)

The previous methods of enforcing data integrity user-defined
> datatypes, defaults, rules and triggers are still available

Constraints can be applied to either columns or tables

Constraints achieve the same functionality
> without requiring separate definition or
> additional steps to bind them

Constraints are stored in the:
- *syscomments*
- *sysreferences*
- *sysconstraints*
- *systems tables*

How to obtain information about Constraints

Run sp_helpconstraint *tablename* in iSQLw to get a report
> (or sp_help *tablename* for full report)

Example: run on *pubs*
> **sp_helpconstraint titles**

Any constraint violation causes the current statement
> to terminate (NOT the transaction)

Triggers are executed after all the constraints have been evaluated

Advantages of constraints

You can place a particular constraint on more than one column
You can place more than one constraint on a column
You can enforce referential integrity with constraints

Limits:
Constraints on a table can include a table- or column-level constraint(s)
- where there are at most, one PRIMARY KEY per table
- no more than 249 UNIQUE constraints
- no more than 31 FOREIGN KEY constraints per table
    (each of which can reference at most 16 columns)
- one DEFAULT constraint per column
- any number of CHECK constraints

All can be entered within the same CREATE TABLE statement

9D.1 Defining Constraints (and Dropping)

Because a constraint is separate from a table's data structure you can
    create & drop constraints without having to drop and recreate tables

Constraints are defined in:
- the CREATE TABLE statement or
- the ALTER TABLE statement
- SQL Enterprise manager

Note: From SQL Ent Mgr Choose: Manage\Tables and hit the

button **+** to access the Advanced Features including constraints

(expand the window to see the whole form)

(click the **+** button to return)

Constraints cannot be altered - they must be dropped and recreated

Syntax of check constraint:

    CREATE TABLE *table_name*
    col_name col_properties constraint constraint

Example of check constraint:

    CREATE TABLE *inventory*
    Item_number int NOT NULL
    constraint Item_number check(item_number < 1000)

This constraint checks that the item_number column value <1000

When a *table* is dropped all system table entries are removed

Creating at table definition time

Examples:
The CREATE TABLE statement for the *authors* table in the *pubs* database.

```
CREATE TABLE authors
(
au_id          id
CHECK (au_id like '[0-9][0-9][0-9]-[0-9][0-9]-[0-9][0-9][0-9][0-9]')
CONSTRAINT UPKCL_auidind PRIMARY KEY CLUSTERED,
    au_lname    varchar(40)    NOT NULL,
    au_fname    varchar(20)    NOT NULL,
    phone       char(12)       NOT NULL
        DEFAULT ('UNKNOWN'),
    address     varchar(40)    NULL,
    city        varchar(20)    NULL,
    state       char(2)        NULL,
    zip         char(5)        NULL
        CHECK (zip like '[0-9][0-9][0-9][0-9][0-9]'),
    contract    bit            NOT NULL
)
```

Note: id is a used-defined data type

Syntax to drop a constraint:
    ALTER TABLE
    DROP constraint_name

9D.2   Implementing Constraints

Constraints can be

1	placed on either a column or a table
2	column constraints improve the readability of data
3	multiple-column constraints are created at table level
4	multiple column-constraints can be placed on a single column
5	placed on a self referencing table
6	created at table definition time
7	added to a table with existing data

Column-level constraints are defined on a single column
and can only be defined in the CREATE TABLE statement

Example: The following CHECK constraint enforces a numeric entry with the format of ### - ## - ####

```
CREATE TABLE authors
( au_id id
CHECK (au_id like '[0-9][0-9][0-9]-[0-9][0-9]-[0-9][0-9][0-9][0-9]')
CONSTRAINT UPKCL_auidind PRIMARY KEY CLUSTERED etc )
```

Table-level constraints are constraints that are defined on >1 column
and can be defined in either the CREATE TABLE statement
or with the ALTER TABLE statements

Example: The following constraint adds a UNIQUE combination-constraint on the *stor_name* and *city* columns

```
ALTER TABLE stores
ADD        CONSTRAINT U_NC_stname_city
           UNIQUE NONCLUSTERED (stor_name, city)
```

Note: The ADD keyword must be used with the ALTER TABLE statement when adding a constraint

Adding constraints to existing data

When a constraint is added the existing data is automatically checked to see if it meets the constraint

The 'WITH NOCHECK' option switches off checking the existing data

Syntax:

```
ALTER TABLE table_name
ADD    CONSTRAINT constraint_name
       PRIMARY KEY (column_name)
```

Example:

```
ALTER TABLE authors
ADD    CONSTRAINT UPKCL_auidind
       PRIMARY KEY CLUSTERED (au_id)
```

9D.3 Types of Constraint

There are 3 general types of constraints
    which each have a different pattern of syntax

        1   Primary key and Unique constraints
        2   Check & Default type constraints
        3   Referential Integrity constraints

These general groups can be divided into:

        1a   Unique constraints
        1b   Primary key constraints
        2a   Check constraints
        2b   Default constraints
        3   Referential Integrity constraints

9D.3a.1 Unique constraints

The UNIQUE constraint can enforce integrity on a non-primary key
They ensure that:
    - no duplicates are entered
    - only one NULL value is allowed
    - an index is created automatically

Are enforced by the creation of a Unique index on the specified
    columns (can be either CLUSTERED or NONCLUSTERED),
    non-clustered by default

Syntax:
CONSTRAINT constraint_name
[UNIQUE] [CLUSTERED|NONCLUSTERED] (col_name, col2_name etc)

Example:
    ALTER TABLE member
    ADD CONSTRAINT U_member_MemberNo
    UNIQUE NONCLUSTERED (MemberNo)

Rules:

One NULL is allowed (unlike in a Primary key) but is not advisable

Can be created on a single column or at the table level for
    multiple columns (composite unique key)

Default = NONCLUSTERED unless the index type is specified

You can only have one Unique index per table

Specifying WITH NOCHECK does not prevent checking for uniqueness

If an INSERT or UPDATE violates the UNIQUE requirements of the index a 'creation violation' message is received (not a general index 'insert error' message)

9D.3a.2 Primary key constraints

You can create a primary key by defining a PRIMARY KEY constraint when you create or alter a table

You can use PRIMARY KEY constraints to enforce both:
- entity integrity   (no duplicate entries)
- referential integrity   (works in conjunction with a REFERENCES constaint on FOREIGN keys)

A PRIMARY KEY constraint ensures that
- no duplicate values are entered
- NULL values are not allowed
- a unique **clustered** index is automatically created

A Primary Key has the same characteristics as a Unique constraint except it does not allow NULL

Syntax:
```
CONSTRAINT       constraint_name
PRIMARY KEY [CLUSTERED|NONCLUSTERED] (col_name,
col2_name etc)
```

Example:
```
ALTER TABLE       member
ADD

CONSTRAINT  PK_member_MemberNo
PRIMARY KEY CLUSTERED (MemberNo)
```

Rules:

Can be created on a column or at the table level for
    multiple columns (composite primary key)

Are enforced by the automatic creation of a Unique index on the
    specified columns

Default = CLUSTERED unless:
    NONCLUSTERED is specified
    A CLUSTERED index already exists on the table

A Primary key index is not visible to users and cannot be 'dropped'
    It is dropped when the PRIMARY KEY constraint is dropped

Can only be placed on a column defined as NOT NULL

Can only have one Primary Key per table
This can be at either the table OR the column level

If a PRIMARY KEY or
    UNIQUE constraint or
    CLUSTERED index
        exists it will have to be dropped before adding
            a new Primary Key (a message appears
                "Cannot add a duplicate PRIMARY KEY")

Tables used for replication require a Primary Key

Can only add a Primary Key to a new column if the IDENTITY
    property is specified

Specifying WITH NOCHECK does not prevent checking
    for uniqueness

9D.3b.1 CHECK constraints

A CHECK constraint determines values that can be entered in a column, or a column with a particular user type, thus it enforces domain integrity

The CHECK constraint is similar to a rule
but does not have to be bound to a column.
It automatically applies to data at the DBMS level

Syntax: ALTER TABLE table_name
ADD
CONSTRAINT constraint_name
CHECK (expression)

Examples of column level constraint:

1. ALTER TABLE authors
ADD
CONSTRAINT CK_zip
CHECK (zip LIKE '[0-9] [0-9] [0-9] [0-9] [0-9]')

Note: the ADD keyword

To create a CHECK constraint

In SQL Enterprise Manager:
Choose Select the Database e.g. Pubs
then Select from the menu: Manage\Tables
Select (1xClk) the table from the drop-down list,
Select (1xClk) the Advanced Features button
(you have to look carefully), and then
Select (1xClk) the Check Constraints tab.
Or
Use CREATE TABLE or ALTER TABLE statement

Rules for CHECK constraints:

Can be created on a column or at the table level for multiple columns (composite primary key)

Are enforced by the creation of a Unique index on the specified columns

Chapter 9 – Data Integrity

Are checked **every** time an UPDATE or INSERT is performed

Cannot be placed on timestamp or IDENTITY columns

Can have multiple CHECKS on the same column

Default is CLUSTERED unless:
- NONCLUSTERED is specified
- A CLUSTERED index already exists on the table

Are dropped when the PRIMARY KEY is dropped

Can only be placed on a column defined as NOT NULL

There can only be one Primary Key per table

CHECK constraints can coexist with a rule on a column

If a

PRIMARY KEY or
UNIQUE constraint or
CLUSTERED index
exists it will have to be dropped before adding a new Primary Key
(a message appears "Cannot add a duplicate PRIMARY KEY")

Note: Tables used for replication require a Primary Key
You can only add a Primary Key to a new column if the IDENTITY property is specified

Specifying the WITH NOCHECK option does not prevent checking for uniqueness but does prevent the CHECK constraint from validating existing data

CHECK can reference other columns in the same table
(Rules cannot)

Can contain a user specified search condition

Cannot contain Subqueries

Example of a table level constraint:

    ADD CONSTRAINT total_gross_pay
        CHECK (total_salary >= base_salary + annual_bonus)

Note: a table level constraint can reference more than 1 column

9D.3b.2 DEFAULTS (2 types)

Defaults can be created at the Column or the Table level

There is some confusion between the two but, briefly, there is a basic difference between:
- a table-level constraint (created in the CREATE TABLE)
- a bound constraint (created with CREATE DEFAULT)

The preferred method is for a table-level constraint to be created
in the CREATE TABLE statement (to enforce domain integrity)
- It does not have to be bound.
- It is removed when the table is dropped

Example:
ALTER TABLE employee
ADD CONSTRAINT DF_SSNo DEFAULT '000-000- 0000'
FOR soc_sec_no

Note: When a bound DEFAULT is created, the column to which it applies is specified with FOR column_name (as above)

In contrast, a DEFAULT can be created
by the CREATE DEFAULT statement
as an object
which can be bound to a column
the same default can be bound to multiple columns

Syntax:
   CREATE DEFAULT default_name
   AS constant_expression

Example:
   CREATE DEFAULT def_ssn
   AS '000-000- 0000'

After the default is created it has to be bound to the column
   e.g.
   sp_bindefault *defname,* *'table_name.column_name'*

sp_bindefault def_ssn, 'employees.ssn'

A default is the value that is entered into a column
   if a user does not enter one
Is associated with a column (not a datatype)
There can be only one default to a column
They cannot be placed on timestamp or IDENTITY columns

They allows the use of system supplied values (Niladic functions)
e.g.   USER
       CURRENT_USER
       SESSION_USER
       SYSTEM_USER
       CURRENT_TIMESTAMP

Example:
> **ALTER TABLE sales_table**
> **ADD**
> **CONSTRAINT def_salesman DEFAULT USER**
> **FOR salesman**

This will cause the niladic function, USER, to be the default named
   def_salesman to be defined for the *salesman* field in the sales table

If a NOT NULL is specified but not a default then
   whenever a user fails to enter a value in a column defined as
   NOT NULL, an error message is returned

9D.3c Foreign Key Constraint (REFERENCES)

A *foreign key* is a column or combination of columns whose values match the primary key of another table

A table can have a maximum of 31 FOREIGN KEY references.

This limit is an absolute upper limit,
but the maximum may be lower depending on the number of work tables the server has to create to enforce the constraint, and the limit varies by the type of query being executed.

FOREIGN KEY constraints are not enforced for temporary tables.

FOREIGN KEY constraints, unlike PRIMARY KEY constraints,
do not create an index.

To improve performance for data retrieval operations, use the CREATE INDEX statement to create an index on a foreign key column

This will allow quicker execution times when a referenced key is modified

For a FOREIGN KEY to be successfully created, the user must have SELECT or REFERENCES permission on the column or columns to which the FOREIGN KEY refers

Foreign key values must be copies of the primary key values

A foreign key doesn't have to be unique

Supplies referential integrity by being matched with the PRIMARY KEY of the 'child' table

You can create a foreign key by defining a FOREIGN KEY constraint when you create or alter a table

Uses a single column or a multi column reference to another table

Is used in conjunction with the REFERENCES constraint

The key may comprise of more than one column

Syntax:

```
ALTER TABLE      table_name
[ADD CONSTRAINT  constraint_name]
FOREIGN KEY      (col_name, [col_name2, . . . col_name16])
REFERENCES       ref_table(ref_col), . . .ref_table16(ref_col16)
```

Example:
```
ALTER TABLE        titles
ADD CONSTRAINT     Pub_Id
FOREIGN KEY        (Pub_Id)
REFERENCES         Publisher(Pub_Id)
```

The Titles table has a constraint that only allows
>an Pub_Id which is listed in the Publishers table

Rules:

The number of columns and the datatypes specified in the
>FOREIGN KEY statement must match the number of
>columns and the datatypes in the REFERENCES clause
>and must be listed in the same order

Can reference the PRIMARY KEY or a UNIQUE constraint
>of another table
>and thereby enforce Domain Integrity

An index is not automatically created on a FOREIGN KEY but
>it is recommended for join performance

Specifying the WITH NOCHECK option will prevent the
>FOREIGN KEY from validating existing data

Order of Processing

1. rules
2. REFERENCES
3. CHECK
4. referenced by
5. triggers

Thus constraints are processed before triggers

However, if you need cross database referential integrity,
>you must use triggers (See Chapter 11)
>>because REFERENCES can only reference items in the same database

REFERENCES constraints require that data added to a table must
>have a matching value in the table it references

E.G. If a sales table has a REFERENCES to the inventory item in the Inventory table then only items that are listed in the Inventory table can be sold

4D.4   When to use Data Integrity Constraints

The trade-offs are functionality & dependencies **vs** performance

The simplest method is always a good place to start so -

First consider, (in this order):
- *1* st   System Datatypes
- *2* nd   NULL or NOT NULL
- *3* rd   User-defined Datatype
- *4* th   Declarative Referential Integrity (Foreign keys & REFERENCES)
- *5* th   Constraints

These are dependent on the column or table as part of the schema
therefore they are neither flexible nor independent,
they cannot be used in any other part of the database
but they are efficient and fast

They are checked before a transaction begins and if a violation occurs an error message appears before an entry is made in the transaction log.

This means errors have less impact on performance

Secondly, consider Rules and defaults
are slightly more independent
can be applied to any columns in the database
they are fast and efficient
but incur a little more overhead

Finally, Triggers and Stored Procedures provide all the functionality you want such as:
- application logic
- looping
- error handling
- ability to reference external data
- tailored error messages

but data integrity checking is done after a transaction has been logged and has to be rolled back if an error

Note: you have to create a datatype, which will be used in a table before creating the table

Type of Integrity	Use - (Type of Constraint)	Other Ways to Implement Integrity
Entity	PK NOT NULL UNIQUE	UNIQUE indexes IDENTITY datatype
Referential	REFERENCES FK	Triggers Stored Procedures
Domain	NOT NULL DEFAULT CHECK User defined datatypes Triggers Stored Procedures	Datatypes Rules Defaults
User defined	REFERENCES FK CHECK	Rules Triggers Stored Procedures

4D.5 Examples of CREATE TABLE statements
with complete table definitions including all constraints
(*jobs*, *employee*, and *publishers* as created in the *pubs* database)

```
CREATE TABLE job
    (
    job_id          smallint        IDENTITY(1,1)
                                    PRIMARY KEY  CLUSTERED,
    job_desc        varchar(50)     NOT NULL
                                    DEFAULT 'New Position –
                                            title not formalized yet',
    min_lvl tiny    int             NOT NULL
                                    CHECK (min_lvl >= 10),
    max_lvl tiny    int             NOT NULL
                                    CHECK (max_lvl <= 250)
    )

CREATE TABLE employee
    (
    emp_id    empid  CONSTRAINT PK_emp_id PRIMARY KEY
    NONCLUSTERED
                    CONSTRAINT CK_emp_id
                    CHECK (emp_id LIKE
                    '[A-Z][A-Z][A-Z][1-9][0-9][0-9][0-9][0-9][FM]'
                    OR emp_id LIKE '[A-Z]-[A-Z][1-9][0-9][0-9][0-9][0-9][FM]'),
    fname           varchar(20)     NOT NULL,
    minit           char(1)         NULL,
    lname           varchar(30)     NOT NULL,
    job_id          smallint        NOT NULL
                                    DEFAULT 1
                                    REFERENCES jobs(job_id),
    job_lvl         tinyint         DEFAULT 10,
    pub_id          char(4)         NOT NULL
                                    DEFAULT ('9952')
                                    REFERENCES publishers(pub_id),
    hire_date       datetime        NOT NULL
                                    DEFAULT (getdate())
    )
```

```
CREATE TABLE publisher
(
pub_id              char(4)         NOT NULL
            CONSTRAINT UPKCL_pubind PRIMARY KEY CLUSTERED
            CHECK (pub_id IN ('1389', '0736', '0877', '1622', '1756')
            OR pub_id LIKE '99[0-9][0-9]'),
pub_name varchar(40)                NULL,
city                varchar(20)     NULL,
state               char(2)         NULL,
country             varchar(30)     NULL    DEFAULT('USA')
)
```

CLIFF'S Step x Step SQL Server

Chapter 10 – Stored Procedures

This chapter is about one of the most powerful features of SQL Server, its ability to store a routine on the server so that it can be called from an application and run on the server.

This keeps network traffic to a minimum and enables speed and consistency from all parts of the network. Also a SP is not run from workstations which may be all sorts of machines and therefore have inconsistent performance. They can also be called over an internet connection.

Readers might ask - why is this chapter not longer, if the subject is so important.

The answer is that this chapter is about creating and using a stored procedure. Programming, which is the content of the stored procedure is the subject of other chapters and even other books, is inappropriate here.

This module is designed to provide an overview of stored procedures
1	Create a stored procedure
2	Describe the execution plan of a stored procedure

Chapter 10:
Stored Procedures

Outline - Context Tool

1	**What is a Stored Procedure**	5
	1A Using Stored Procedures	6
	1B Benefits of using Stored Procedures	7
	1C Stored Procedures are Independent	7
2	**Creating Stored Procedures**	8
3	**Rules and Guidelines**	10
4	**Parameters**	11

10.1   What is a Stored Procedure?

A Stored Procedure is a set of precompiled SQL statements
      which can include control-of-flow statements
      stored on the server (with a name)
      which can be executed as a unit
      by a call to its name.

They allow:
      - user-declared variables
      - conditional execution

Stored procedures supplied by SQL Server are called system stored procedures

System stored procedure scripts are stored in the master database in the sysprocedures table
except for Events, Alerts and Tasks which are stored in the MSDB database since they relate to functions common to the server

The text which creates them is stored in the syscomments table

procedure_names must:

- conform to the rules for identifiers and
- must be unique within the database and its owner.

You can create local or global temporary procedures
      by preceding the *procedure_name* with:
 - a single pound sign (#*table_name*) for local temporary procedures and
 - a double pound sign (##*table_name*) for global temporary procedures.
The complete name, including # or ##, cannot exceed 20 characters.

10.1A Using Stored Procedures

They are checked for syntax, optimized and compiled the first time they
   are executed

They remain in the procedure cache until replaced
   by a another procedure

They are invoked by the application - not by SQL Server

They are called by merely using their name
   (use **execute** keyword if it is not the first statement in the batch)

They can either modify data or retrieve data - not both at once

Can be created for:
- *permanent use*
   are retained in the database until dropped
- *as a local temporary procedure*
   (temporary use within *a* user's session)
   named with the # first character and
   lasts only for the duration of the connection to the server
- *global temporary procedure*
   (temporary use within *all* user's sessions)
   named with ## as the first characters and
   lasts only while there is any connection to the server

Can execute automatically on startup of SQL Server

Syntax
sp_makestartup *procedure_name*

Where procedure_name specifies the name of the procedure to start
   automatically when the server is started.

Permanent stored procedures are stored as a database object
   in the syscomments systems table
   and can be listed by running sp_helptext

Syntax:
> execute MyServer.MyDatabase.dbo.sp_name

Example:
> execute MyServer.MyDatabase.dbo.sp_byroyalty 25

Example step 1: In a new query in pubs, type:
> **byroyalty   25**

the byroyalty stored procedure will ruturn a list of au_id's for all the authors with a 25% royalty rate

Example step 2: In the pubs database, type:
> **sp_helptext byroyalty**

this will list the code in the byroyalty stored procedure from the syscomments table

10.1B Benefits of using Stored procedures

They are fast and efficient

They enforces consistency

They encapsulate business functionality (for use by applications)

Changes to business rules and policies require only the SP to be changed

They can share logic with other applications (Modular programming)

They reduce network traffic because they are stored and executed on the server

Can take and return user-supplied parameters

A user can be granted permission for a SP even if not on the tables and views referenced by it. Therefore it can be used as a security mechanism

Restricted 'function based' access to the database is possible by granting permissions to use particular SPs

10.1C Stored Procedures are independent

SQL Query	**Stored Procedure Call**
(from app)	(from app)
Parse	Locate Procedure
Validation	
Check Protection	Check Protection
Optimize	Substitute Parameters
Compile	**Execute**

10.2 Creating a Stored Procedure

You can create a Stored Procedure only in the current database
(except temporary SPs which are created in tempdb)

Simple Syntax:
> CREATE PROC stored_procedure_name
> AS
> > SQL Statements
>
> RETURN

Example:
> CREATE PROC sproc_pub_titles
> AS
> > SELECT p.pub_name, t.title
> > FROM publishers p, titles t
> > WHERE p.pub_id = t.pub_id
>
> RETURN

Complete Syntax:
> CREATE PROC [owner.]stored_procedure_name [;number]
> > [(parameter1, parameter2, . . parameter255)]
> > [FOR REPLICATION | WITH RECOMPILE]
> > [ENCRYPTION]
>
> AS
> > SQL Statements
>
> RETURN

Note: Nesting of SPs is allowed to 16 levels
(in other words, a stored procedure can call another stored procedure)
Parameters are optional
Parameter values are supplied by the user at execution time
Using the OUTPUT parameter returns a value to the user
The number option is used to group SPs of the same name
   sproc_one:1, sproc_one:2, sproc_one:3, etc
Only use ENCRYPTION where absolutely necessary

10.2A Dropping a Stored Procedure

Syntax:
DROP PROC sproc_name

Example:
DROP PROC sproc_pub_titles

When you drop an SP information about it is removed from the sysobjects, sysprocedures and syscomments files

A whole group can be dropped but not individual members of a group

10.2B Running a Stored Procedure

First Execution	Subsequent executions
Locate	Locate
Substitute Parameters	Substitute Parameters
Develop Optimization Plan	
Compile	
Execute from cache	Execute from cache

Private and Public temporary SPs are similar to temporary tables
You create temporary procedures with the # sign
    a single # for local   **e.g. #proc_name**
    a double # for global   **e.g. ##proc_name**
A SP name has Max 20 characters

10.2C Dropping a Stored Procedure

Syntax:
DROP PROC sproc_name

Example:
DROP PROC sproc_pub_titles

When you drop an SP information about it is removed from the sysobjects, sysprocedures and syscomments files

A whole group can be dropped but not individual members of a group

Running a Stored Procedure

First Execution	Subsequent executions
Locate	Locate
Substitute Parameters	Substitute Parameters
Develop Optimization Plan	
Compile	
Execute from cache	Execute from cache

Private and Public temporary SPs are similar to temporary tables

You create temporary procedures with the # sign
    a single # for local   e.g. #proc_name
    a double # for global   e.g. ##proc_name

A SP name has Max 20 characters

10.3   Rules and Guidelines

1 You cannot reference a non existent object

2 You can have an unlimited number of variables in a SP

3 The CREATE PROC statement can include unlimited number of SQL statements

4 The following are not allowed:
   CREATE VIEW
   CREATE TRIGGER
   CREATE DEFAULT
   CREATE PROC
   CREATE RULE

5 Within a SP objects with the same name cannot be created, dropped or recreated

6 You can reference temporary tables (local & global) created in the SP and global temporary tables created outside the SP but local temporary tables disappear when the SP finishes

Information on Stored Procedures
Use sp_helptext SP_name

   e.g. exec sp_helptext sproc_pub_titles

Also use *sp_depends* for a report on the objects referenced

   e.g. exec sp_depends sproc_pub_titles

Tip:
   When writing SPs first test the SQL statements

10.4 Parameters

When a procedure calls another procedure, the called procedure
    can use objects created by the calling procedure

This is done be defining parameters in CREATE PROC

@parameter_name specifies a parameter in a procedure (max 255)

The user must supply the value of each declared parameter when
    the SP is executed (unless a default is defined)

Syntax:

Several formats are used in the CREATE PROC statement:

1   @parameter_name datatype

2   @parameter_name datatype = [default | NULL]

3   @parameter_name datatype [= default | NULL] [OUTPUT]

by using the OUTPUT option,
    values for the parameters are retained after the SP finishes
This is referred to as a "pass by reference" capability
    and the variable can be used in additional SQL statements
    in the batch or in the calling procedure

Parameters can be passed:

- by position
  EXEC proc_name (value1| @variable, value2 | @variable, etc)
  which has to be then referenced in the same order as
  they were listed in the create statement

- or by name
  EXEC proc_name
      @parameter1 = value|@variable
      @parameter2 = value|@variable
      @parameter3 = value|@variable
  which can be referenced in any order

Example:
```
CREATE PROC titles_sum
@title varchar(40) = '%', @sum money output
```

CLIFF'S Step x Step SQL Server

Chapter 11 - Triggers

A *trigger* is a special kind of stored procedure that goes into effect
(i.e. is automatically invoked) whenever a specified event modifies a table including:
- **UPDATE**
- **INSERT**
- **DELETE**

A trigger is executed once per SQL statement but can "fire" either:

1. immediately **after** the data modification statements are completed - or
2. Before the event (it is actually referred to as an "Instead of" trigger

Triggers are often created to enforce business rule consistency among logically related data in different tables

An advantage of triggers is that they are automatic
    they work no matter what caused the data modification
e.g. a clerk's entry or an application action

In performance terms, trigger overhead is usually low

The time involved in running a trigger is spent mostly in referencing other tables which can be either in memory or on the database device

A trigger and the statement that fires it are treated as a single transaction that can be rolled back from within the trigger

Triggers use *deleted* and *inserted* tables which are always in memory (RAM)

A trigger can query other tables and it can include complex T-SQL statements

Triggers are primarily useful for enforcing complex business rules or requirements, such as whether to insert an order based on a customer's current account status

Triggers are useful for:
- enforcing referential integrity,
- preserving the defined relationships between tables whenever you enter or delete records in those tables.

However, the best way to enforce referential integrity is to define FOREIGN KEY constraints

Introduction to Triggers

This module is designed to enable you to:

1. Explain what triggers are
2. Explain the difference between triggers and stored procedures
3. Create triggers
4. List the items that triggers enforce

Outline - The Context Tool

1	**What is a trigger**	5
2	**Creating and Dropping a trigger**	7
3	**Trigger rules and guidelines**	8
4	**Modification triggers**	9
4A	INSERT trigger	10
4B	DELETE trigger	11
4C	UPDATE trigger	12
5	**Enforcing integrity through triggers**	13
5A	Enforcing data integrity	13
5B	Enforcing referential integrity	14
6	**Multi-row triggers**	15
7	**Business rules**	16
8	**Getting Information about Triggers**	16

11.1 What is a trigger?

A trigger is similar to a stored procedure that is invoked whenever an attempt is made to modify (INSERT, UPDATE, DELETE) the data that it protects

A trigger is an advanced form of a Rule (that can examine data and span multiple tables) used to enforce elaborate
        restrictions on data preventing:
- *unauthorized* or
- *inconsistent*

changes to the data

Triggers are often used to:

a) enforce:

1. business rules
2. complex column-rules (can reference virtually any data in any source)
3. data integrity:
   a. you can cascade updates & deletes of keys (which a constraint cannot do)
   b. other referential integrity requirements supported by constraints
4. complex <u>defaults</u> - derived defaults

b) maintain:

5. updated summary data
6. duplicate data (but replication is a better method)

Triggers are database objects that are bound to <u>tables</u> (unlike stored procedures which are independent of tables)

Some characteristics of Triggers:

1. are automatically invoked by SQL Server
2. cannot be called directly
3. have no parameters
4. can nest to 16 levels

Consider the following when using triggers:

Trigger overhead is low

The *inserted* and *deleted* tables are usually very small
  and they are always in memory

The location of referenced tables determines the time operations take

If an error is detected the transaction rolls back and the original trigger is cancelled

The nested trigger option is automatically set 'on' at installation,
  to disable it use:
    sp_configure 'nested triggers', 0

11.2 Creating and Dropping a trigger

Syntax:
CREATE TRIGGER trigger_name
    ON table_name
    FOR [INSERT | UPDATE | DELETE] [WITH ENCRYPTION]
    AS
        sql statements
        [return]

Example:

```
CREATE TRIGGER Authors_Insert_Trigger
    ON      authors
    FOR INSERT
    AS
            print "Author Inserted"
            return
```

Note:

The SQL statements specify :
- *the table on which the trigger is defined*
- *the events for which the trigger will fire*
  (i.e. INSERT, UPDATE, DELETE)

The actual body of the trigger follows the **AS** keyword
and contains the statements that are executed

The WITH ENCRYPTION option causes the entry in the syscomments file
(contains the text of the trigger) to be encrypted

Dropping Triggers
The only way to prevent a trigger from firing is to DROP it

Syntax:

    DROP TRIGGER trigger_name

11.3 Trigger Rules and Guidelines

Each table can have a maximum of 3 triggers on the actions:

>one INSERT
>one UPDATE
>one DELETE

Each trigger applies to one table only

A single trigger can process up to all 3 actions
>of INSERT, UPDATE & DELETE

A trigger cannot be created on a temporary table or a view but triggers can reference them

A trigger should not include SELECT statements that return results to the user since the returned results would have to be included in every application in which modificatiions to the table

Caveat: If a trigger is defined when there is already a trigger it the original trigger. No warning is given - so beware!

When a table is dropped so are all the triggers with the table

Use **sp_depends** *table_name* to view the details of triggers
>e.g. **sp_depends employee**

This returns:

name	type
dbo.employee_insupd	trigger

Note: Since SQL Server 6.0 triggers REFERENTIAL INTEGRITY does not require a trigger since it is provided in the CREATE TABLE statement

Similarly you cannot use a trigger to drop the row in a table that matches the primary key whenever a Foreign key is defined. A sp_procedure can do this

11.4 Modification Triggers

While triggers resemble stored procedures, triggers
        provide two procedures that are unique
- **1**   the trigger test tables
  - *INSERTED table* and
  - *DELETED table*
- **2**   the IF UPDATE statement

both of these are available only within the body of a trigger

The trigger test tables hold the data from the rows by the event that caused the trigger to fire

The *deleted* table and *inserted* table are logical tables in cache which are structurally like the trigger tables

The INSERTED table contains the rows being inserted and the DELETED table contains the rows being deleted these tables may be used to manage data modification and validation

First, rows are inserted into the table and the *inserted* table, and then the trigger fires Thus it is possible to rollback transactions that are invalid

The IF UPDATE statement allows trigger actions to be associated with updates to **specified columns** by testing whether a particular column in the row is being updated

With INSERT and UPDATE statements the IF statement returns 'true'

The global variable @@ROWCOUNT can be used to return the number of rows that have been modified

Application of a default is the same as any other data modification

Constraints are checked before triggers are fired so if a constraint is violated a trigger is not fired

11.4A INSERT trigger

When you INSERT data SQL Server creates a table in cache that holds the data while processing

    Trigger Table   'Inserted' table
    Original Data   INSERT
    Inserted Data   and Inserted Data

When an INSERT statement is executed, new rows are added to both the trigger table and to the INSERTED table

The INSERTED table can be examined by the trigger to determine how to carry out the trigger actions

An advantage of the INSERTED table is that you can reference data without having to store it in variables

The INSERTED table allows comparison of the inserted rows with the rows in the INSERTED table since the rows in the INSERTED table are always duplicates of the rows in the trigger table

Example:

Create a trigger that sets a flag called 'hired' in the tblitem table when an item is recorded as on hire in the tblhired table

```
CREATE TRIGGER      trig_hired
ON                  tblhired
FOR INSERT
AS
UPDATE              tblitem
SET                 on_hire = "Y"
FROM                item, inserted
WHERE               item.serial_no = inserted.serial_no
```

Further Example:

This insert trigger updates the *ytd_sales* column in the *titles* table each time a new *sales* row is added.

It goes into effect whenever you record a sale by adding a row to the *sales* table.

It updates the *ytd_sales* column in the *titles* table so that *ytd_sales* is equal to its previous value plus the value added to *sales.qty*.

This keeps the totals up to date for inserts into *sales.qty*.

```
CREATE TRIGGER intrig_updateYTDSales
ON              sales
FOR INSERT AS
UPDATE          titles
SET             ytd_sales = ytd_sales + qty
FROM            inserted
WHERE           titles.title_id = inserted.title_id
```

Note Triggers used to maintain summary values should contain GROUP BY clauses to create summary values when more than one row is being inserted, updated, or deleted

Because a GROUP BY clause imposes extra overhead, the following examples are written to test whether the value of @@ROWCOUNT is equal to one, meaning that only one row in the trigger table was affected

If @@ROWCOUNT is equal to one, the trigger actions take effect without a GROUP BY clause.

Another good example is whenever a transaction takes place in a database you can update a 'scoreboard' table of totals.
Of course, this does add to the overhead associated with a transaction.

11.4B DELETE triggers

When you DELETE data, SQL Server creates a table in cache that holds the deleted data while processing

Trigger Table	***Deleted*' table**
Data has gone	**DELETE** Deleted Data
Remaining Data stays	

Note: When data is appended to the deleted table it has already gone from the Trigger table, therefore the tables have no rows in common

The DELETE trigger does not execute for the TRUNCATE TABLE statement

11.4C UPDATE Triggers

An UPDATE is a combination of a DELETE and an INSERT transaction

When an UPDATE statement is executed on a table that has an UPDATE trigger the original rows are deleted (moved to a *deleted* table) and the new data is inserted into both the trigger table and the *inserted* table

Trigger Table   **'Deleted' table**

Data has been
   replaced -   Deleted Data
Data has gone
Inserted Data   **DELETE**
   is here
Other Data

                'Inserted' table
INSERT   Inserted Data

Once the UPDATE statement has executed, (during which the deleted and inserted tables are loaded) - then the UPDATE trigger is fired

The trigger table and the deleted and inserted tables can be examined by the trigger to determine whether multiple rows have been updated and how the trigger actions should be carried out

IF UPDATE

In addition you can define a trigger to test modifications to a specific

```
CREATE TRIGGER trig_pub_id
ON              publishers
FOR INSERT
AS
   IF UPDATE(pub_id)
   BEGIN
          RAISERROR ('Transaction cannot be processed
               Pub_id cannot be changed',10,1)
          ROLLBACK TRANSACTION
   END
```

The virtual tables (called 'inserted' and 'deleted') are used to determine the values that have been replaced or deleted.

The tables are 'virtual' because they are actually views of the log which are stored in memory

Therefore the data modification can be rolled back:
- if an error is detected
- if a trigger is violated

11.4D AFTER Triggers

An AFTER trigger fires after the event it is associated with (INSERT, UPDATE, DELETE)

A trigger is considered a part of the transaction that includes the event that caused it to fire

The timing of a trigger is determined by replacinging the word FOR with the word AFTER (or the words INSTEAD OF) in your code

Example:
FOR INSERT
AFTER INSERT
INSTEAD OF INSERT

Example (see previous):

Create a trigger that sets a flag called 'hired' in the tblitem table when an item is recorded as on hire in the tblhired table to be triggered after the INSERT event

```
CREATE TRIGGER  trig_hired
ON              tblhired
AFTER INSERT
AS
UPDATE          tblitem
SET             on_hire = "Y"
FROM            item, inserted
WHERE           item.serial_no = inserted.serial_no
```

Further Example (see previous):

This insert trigger updates the *ytd_sales* column in the *titles* table each time a new *sales* row is added to be triggered after the INSERT event

It goes into effect whenever you record a sale by adding a row to the *sales* table

It updates the *ytd_sales* column in the *titles* table so that *ytd_sales* is equal to its previous value plus the value added to *sales.qty*

This keeps the totals up to date for inserts into *sales.qty*

```
CREATE TRIGGER intrig_updateYTDSales
ON              sales
AFTER INSERT AS
UPDATE          titles
SET             ytd_sales = ytd_sales + qty
```

11.4E INSTEAD OF Triggers

These triggers fire before the event (INSERT, UPDATE, DELETE)
One of the most common uses of an INSTEAD OF trigger is when a view needs to be updated and that view is based on more than one table. An INSTEAD OF trigger can split the UPDATE into two separate UPDATE statements for each table underlying the view

Also they can be used when you want to use a trigger to enforce uniqueness.

For example:

```
CREATE TRIGGER iotrig_categoryname
ON category
INSTEAD OF INSERT
AS
BEGIN
SET NOCOUNT ON    --(see note below)
IF EXISTS (
SELECT COUNT(*)
       FROM Inserted
       GROUP BY category
       HAVING COUNT(*) > 1
)
BEGIN
       THROW 50000, 'Duplicate Category', 0
       END
ELSE
INSERT  category(category, description)
END
```

Note: NOCOUNT means No Count – to set NOCOUNT ON means that the automatic count of the number of lines affected is turned off – this means that the number of rows affected are NOT counted and therefore, not returned to the calling procedure

11.5 Enforcing integrity with triggers

Triggers may be used to enforce:
1. Data Integrity
2. Referential Integrity
3. Business Rules

While much of the work done with triggers may be better
accomplished through constraints, triggers are needed to enforce Business Rules

11.5A Enforcing data integrity

Triggers can be used to enforce data integrity by cascading changes throughout the database
In order to maintain duplicate data (or derived data) triggers are typically required

Example:
When an on hire item is returned and deleted from the on hire table

```
CREATE TRIGGER trig_hire_delete
ON              tblhired
FOR DELETE
AS
    UPDATE      tblitem
    SET on_hire `= "N"
    FROM        item, deleted
    WHERE       item.serial_no = deleted.serial_no
```

Note:
Since version 6.0 triggers are not required to enforce referential integrity.
Referential Integrity is provided in the CREATE TABLE statement

Similarly you cannot use a trigger to drop the row matching a
Primary Key in another table whenever a row with a Foriegn Key is defined
You would do this with a stored procedure.

11.5B   Enforcing Referential integrity

Referential Integrity can be defined by using FOREIGN KEY constraints and REFERENCE constraints in the CREATE TABLE statement

Triggers can ensure appropriate actions are taken when cascading deletions or updates are needed

Constraints are checked first on the trigger table and if they are violated the trigger is not run

Example: Validating a Foreign key

```
CREATE TRIGGER     trig_titles_insert
ON                 titles
FOR INSERT
AS
   IF (SELECT COUNT (*)
       FROM        publishers, inserted
       WHERE       publishers.pub_id = inserted.pub_id) = 0

       BEGIN
           PRINT 'Transaction cannot be processed'
           PRINT 'No entry in Publishers for this Title'
           ROLLBACK TRANSACTION
       END
```

BEGIN TRANS is implied when a ROLLBACK TRANSACTION is used in a trigger

Note: triggers are fired after data is modified but the transaction can be rolled back

Triggers can reference tables in other databases by using the full identifier

Example: Validating a value against an external table

```
CREATE TRIGGER    zip_check
ON                authors
AFTER INSERT, UPDATE
AS
IF NOT EXISTS
```

```
(SELECT         geodata . . zipcodes.zip
FROM            geodate . . zipcodes, inserted
WHERE           geodate . . zipcodes = inserted.zip
)
BEGIN
        PRINT 'Zipcode Bad'
        ROLLBACK TRANSACTION
END
```

11.6 Multi row trigger

Multi row modifications can occur from SELECT statements

They may require a different treatment/response from a trigger

Example:
Validating Foreign keys for a multiple update statement

```
CREATE TRIGGER trig_titles_insert
ON              titles
AFTER INSERT
AS
DECLARE @rowcnt int
SELECT          @rowcnt = @@rowcount
    IF      (SELECT COUNT (*)
            FROM        publishers, inserted
            WHERE       publishers.pub_id = inserted.pub_id) = 0
                BEGIN
                        PRINT 'Transaction cannot be processed'
                        PRINT 'No entry in Publishers for this Title'
                        ROLLBACK TRANSACTION
                END
    IF      (SELECT COUNT (*)
            FROM        publishers, inserted
            WHERE       publishers.pub_id = inserted.pub_id) <> 0
                BEGIN
                        PRINT 'Transactions cannot be processed'
                        PRINT 'Not all Titles have a valid pub_id in Publishers'
                        ROLLBACK TRANSACTION
                END
```

Note: Notice that control-of-flow language is fully supported in triggers

Note 2: the inserted table and the deleted virtual tables can be referenced

11.7 Business rules

If you wish to delete a publisher you may want to check to ensure they have no titles in inventory

Example:

A DELETE statement such as:
```
DELETE      publisher
WHERE       pub_name = "ABC Publishing"
```

may fire a trigger attached to the publishers table:
```
CREATE TRIGGER    trig_publisher_delete
ON                publishers
AFTER DELETE
AS
    IF
    (
        SELECT COUNT (*)
        FROM        publishers, deleted
        WHERE       titles.pub_id = deleted.pub_id
    ) = 0
    BEGIN
        PRINT 'Transaction cannot be processed'
        PRINT 'This publisher still has titles in inventory'
        ROLLBACK TRANSACTION
    END
```

bcp

When bcp is used to copy data into a table, triggers are ignored.
To compensate for this, business rules should be checked by running a query or stored procedure against the table.

e.g. the query:
```
UPDATE  titles
SET     title = title
```
would not change the data but it would cause an UPDATE trigger to fire against every row in the table

11.8   Getting Information about Triggers

The text of a trigger is stored in the syscomments table

To see the text use:
>   **sp_helptext** *trigger_name*

Example:
>   **sp_helptext employee_insupd**

Chapter 12 – Indexes

Normalizing Logical Database Design

Normalizing a logical database design involves using formal methods to separate the data into multiple, related tables. A greater number of narrow tables (with fewer columns) is characteristic of a *normalized database*.
A few wide tables (with more columns) is characteristic of an *unnormalized database*.
Reasonable normalization will often improve performance. When 'useful' indexes are available, the SQL Server optimizer is very efficient at selecting rapid, efficient joins between a reasonable number of tables.
These are some of the benefits of normalization:
- Faster sorting and index creation because tables are narrower.
- More 'clustered' indexes are allowed because there are more tables.
- Narrower and more compact indexes.
- Fewer indexes per table, helping INSERT, UPDATE and DELETE performance.
- Fewer NULLs and less redundant data, increasing database compactness.
- Improved concurrency when running DBCC diagnostics, because the necessary table locks will affect less data.

As normalization increases, so will the number and complexity of joins required to retrieve data. Too many complex relational joins between too many tables can hinder performance. Reasonable normalization often includes very few regularly executed queries that use more than four-way joins.
Sometimes the logical database design is already fixed and total redesign is not feasible. Even then, however, it might be possible to selectively normalize a large table into several smaller tables. If access to the database is conducted through stored procedures, this schema change could take place without affecting applications. If not, it might be possible to create a view that hides the schema change from the applications.

Note: The term CLUSTERED index refers to the situation where the data is stored in the same sequential order as the index. It is obviously faster to find an item if that item is stored sequentially, rather like the Telephone Directory when we had such book (in the old days) – alphabetical order – it is easier to look up a number if the data is stored (or printed) in the alphabetical order of the names field. However a name field is not a good candidate for a PK – it needs to be unique - a Primary key field has such a Clustered Index (a PK is unique by definition). See later for a more in depth discussion.

Chapter 12:

INDEXES

There are probably more performance problems fixed by correct Indexing than any other method. Sub-second response is the ultimate goal of any OLTP system.

Some other common techniques in tuning databases include:
- the design of the logical database
- physical factors
- hardware bottlenecks and resource usage
- lock contentions
- integrity factors (greater required consistency results in a
    greater performance hit)
- the mix of OLTP and DSS database activities

but the greatest and most common of these is effective Indexing. Indexing is also one of the easiest solutions and at the same time the most difficult to fix if you do not have a proper understanding of how SQL Server applies its logic in choosing whether to use an Index. The correct choice of Index by the query optimizer can have dramatic results (it has also been described as 'sensational').

Imagine if you had no Index on a reference book and the data was not arranged in any order (such as alphabetic). How would you find the section that you wanted to read. Well, the only way would be to scan the whole book, usually starting at the front (but not necessarily if you are right handed) and look for a keyword or some other key that would attract your eye. If it was not indeed in the book you would have to scan the whole book in order to ascertain that what you were looking for was not there. Computers work the same way (but with the added efficiency of doing the scan completely accurately and only having to look once). If you could find a key in the index (which is arranged in order) you can turn to the page immediately, thereby saving a huge effort. Computers work the same way.

Unlike a book, which usually only has one index a table in a database can have multiple indexes which can be of different types.

Note: Only one index can be used per table in each query

> **Caveat:** Before you go out and start attaching every conceivable index to every table you might want to read this chapter

Chapter 12:

This Chapter is designed to enable you to:
- Understand why and when you would use an Index
- Create different types of Indexes
- Understand some of the performance implications of Indexes

INDEXES
Outline - The Context Tool

1	**When to use Indexes**	5
1A	Reasons for using Indexes	6
1B	Reasons for not Indexing	6
1C	Initial Guidelines for Indexing	7
1D	Columns that should not be Indexed	7
2	**Creating an Index**	8
2A	The Rules	8
2B	Duplicate Rows and Keys	8
3	**Types of Index**	10
3A	Clustered	10
3B	Non-clustered	12
4	**Characteristics of Indexes**	14
4A	Unique 14	
4B	Composite	15
5	**Performance Considerations**	16
5A	Index usage	16
5B	Optimizer hints	21
5C	UPDATE STATISTICS	22
5D	Query covering	23
5E	FILLFACTOR	24
5F	SORTED_DATA and SORTED_ DATA_REORG	25
5G	DBCC SHOWCONTIG 26	

12.1   IMPLEMENTING INDEXES

Firstly, what is an Index?

It is a database object that provides access to data in the rows of a table and is based on key values

Specifically, an index is a table that is logically ordered/sorted by the values of a key

Indexes are stored in the same form as data, on index pages that have the same reference methodology as data. They have value ranges that enable a query
to move through a tree-like path to data values instead of having to scan all the rows in a table

Indexes provide quick access to data and also can enforce uniqueness on the rows in a table

The rationale behind indexes is that they can be manipulated at multiple levels much easier than the underlying data which consists of many items of information (fields)

SQL Server supports clustered and nonclustered indexes.
In a clustered index, data is stored in the same order as the index
In a nonclustered index, data is stored in a different order from the index

12.1A Reasons for using Indexes

4 Primary reasons:
1. to enforce the uniqueness of rows
2. speed up data retrieval
3. speed up joins (referential integrity checks)
4. speed up ORDER BY and GROUP BY clauses

Note: They are always created in ascending order
The Query Optimizer depends on Indexes to function

12.1B Reasons for not Indexing

Indexes:
- *1* Take time to create
- *2* Use disk space
- *3* Are dynamically maintained, reflecting changes (Insert, Update, Delete) and therefore they slow the process

There is a conflict between the interests of an OLTP system
>   which requires fast response to the user (typically **sub-second**) and a DSS which requires only an adequate response time (e.g. say up to 20 secs)

An OLTP system usually demands no slow-down and typical complaints about the system involve response time, so anything that will slow the system is not good

A DSS, usually, is there to produce reports and needs only a response time that is not inordinately long. A complex query can run for hours if indexing is inadequate

There is a trade-off between:
>   the interests of fast OLTP response (which can occur 1500 times/day) and
>   a long report time (3 hours) from a DSS (which may only happen once/day)

DON'T INDEX A OLTP DATABASE UNTIL IT CHOKES

Special note about "The Cload"

Advocates of cloud hosting claim fast response BUT this will depend upon outside influences such connection speed. While these speeds are improving, it should be remembered that, typically a user experiences an irritation if response time is not fast. Definitely, any time greater than a second is inadequate and disturbs a user. Data entry by 10-key has to be seen to be appreciated

12.1C Initial Guidelines for Indexing Columns

1   Create Indexes on Columns that are searched frequently
      especially on columns:
- used often in a WHERE clause
- often searched in ranges
- retrieved in sorted order

2   Primary keys should be Indexed uniquely
3   Indexing on columns that are used often in joins can aid
      efficiency of joins especially Foreign key columns
4   Ensure that all tables that do not consist solely of columns that should not be indexed should have at least one index

12.1D Columns that should not be Indexed

The Query Optimizer compares an estimate of the amount of
    work that has to be done using an Index with the work
    if not using an Index

Estimates are based upon statistics
    which are calculated on the first column of the index only

Example:
A column has only M or F as a domain
It would not make sense to use a Nonclustered Index because:
The result set will include a high percentage of rows
    The Index would not be used
It may be advantageous to use a clustered index because the data would be sorted

Rules:
Indexes should not be used on columns that:
1   are seldom referenced in a query
2   contain only a few unique values (use a clustered index)
3   are defined with text, image or bit datatypes and when
      UPDATE is more important than SELECT performance

12.2 Creating an Index

An index is created with the CREATE INDEX statement

Simple Syntax:
```
CREATE INDEX       index_name
ON     table_name (column_name, column_name, . . .)
```

Example:
```
CREATE INDEX       titleindex
ON     titles(title_id)
```

Comprehensive Syntax:
```
CREATE [UNIQUE] [CLUSTERED|NONCLUSTERED]
     INDEX index_name
ON database.owner.table_name (column_name, column_name, . . .)
[ WITH          [PAD_INDEX,]
     [FILLFACTOR = x,]
     [IGNORE_DUP_KEY,]
     [SORTED_DATA|SORTED_DATA_REORG,]
     [IGNORE_DUP_ROW|ALLOW_DUP_ROW] ]
[ON segment_name]
```

Indexes are used by SQL Server optimizer to make queries more efficient

Note: Indexes can be created on tables in other databases
by using a qualifier

The ON clause (when used with a clustered index) causes the whole
table to be placed on the segment
(because the leaf level of a clustered index contains the data)

12.2A Some Index Rules

A clustered Index changes the physical order of items in a table

Only the table Owner can Create /Drop indexes

Indexes can be created/dropped at any time

Create clustered indexes before nonclustered indexes
to avoid rebuilding the nonclustered index

Indexes cannot be created on views or columns with
datatype = bit, image, text

UNIQUE INDEXES

Specified to create a unique index

The system checks for duplicate values when the index is created
    and checks each time data is added with INSERT or UPDATE

If there are duplicate key values, the statement is canceled and
    an error message giving the first duplicate is returned

You cannot create a unique index where the key is NULL in more than one row;
    these are treated as duplicate values for indexing purposes

12.2B Duplicate rows and keys

There is NEVER an occasion where you need duplicate rows,
    the elimination of data redundancy is one of the primary goal of a
    normalized database

However, there can be a situation where duplicates get into a table
- legacy data
- entry/import of data in bulk
- entry by mistake in a non-unique table

The IGNORE_DUP_KEY allows you to delete the duplicates when they
    are encountered

By turning on this option you cause duplicate rows to be deleted from
    either the existing table or from data being inserted

By definition, unique indexes are only used on tables that do not allow
    duplicate rows

If you create an index with the IGNORE_DUP_KEY option active,
    rows with duplicate keys will be ignored/deleted

INDEX	Clustered	Non-clustered
Unique	IGNORE_DUP_KEY IGNORE_DUP_ROW	IGNORE_DUP_KEY IRRELEVANT -
Non-unique	OR ALLOW_DUP_ROW	No inherant restrictions on duplicates

Note:
    IGNORE_DUP_ROW | ALLOW_DUP_ROW
- Are options for creating a nonunique clustered index;
  - they are mutually exclusive
- They only apply when a Clustered Index is non-unique,
  - you can delete the duplicate rows,
  - or
  - allow duplicates in the clustered index (which means they will be stored in adjacent rows since the Clustered index will sort the data into the order of the index)

When creating a nonunique nonclustered index, these options are irrelevant because SQL Server attaches a unique row identification number internally; it will not check for duplicate rows or any other duplicate data

12.3   Types of Indexes

Indexes can be Clustered or Non-clustered
The difference can be thought of as:
    with a clustered index the data is ordered according to
    the sort order defined by the cluster column

12.3A Clustered Indexes

Rows are maintained in a sorted order
The physical order and the indexed order are the same
The 'leaf' level contains the actual data

Illustration of Clustered Indexed Table

Root level

Key	Page
G	100

Node or non-Leaf level

Page 100

Key	Page
G	4
J	5
M	6

Page 101

Key	Page
P	7
S	8
V	9

Leaf level

Page 4	Page 5	Page 6	Page 7	Page 8	Page 9
G	J	M	P	S	V
H	K	N	Q	T	W
I	L	O	R	U	X

Example: Find G

Root		=>	Page 100
Node:	Page 100	=>	Page 4
Leaf:	Page 4	=>	Data for key = G

'CLUSTERED' is NOT the default

There can be only a single clustered index per table
UPDATE and DELETE operations may be accelerated by clustered indexes

Typically, for a table that has at least one index,
> you should make one of those indexes a clustered index

The Primary Key column is always a good candidate for
> consideration as a clustered index
> (but it should also be considered when optimizing)

A clustered index is of advantage when:
- data has a small domain
- data has contiguous values
- columns are often searched for 'ranges' of data

The most important factor is the processing requirements of the user:

1 how do they do their business
2 frequency of queries
3 the characteristics of the data

Consider using a clustered index for:

1. Columns that contain a limited (but not tiny) number of unique values
   E.G: a *state* column of a *customers* table that contains 50
   unique state abbreviations, such as WA, CA, and MO.

2. Queries that return a range of values,
   using operators such as BETWEEN, >, >=, <, and <=.
   E.G. SELECT * FROM sales
   WHERE ord_date BETWEEN '5/1/93' AND '6/1/93'

3. Queries that return large results sets
   E.G: SELECT * FROM phonebook
   WHERE last_name = 'Smith'

Building the Index

The process of building a clustered index takes more than twice the space
> occupied by the table

You have to store:
- the original data

- the new sorted data
- a work area

This means an additional 1.21 times the table size

The space required to build an index is set aside in the database not in tempdb.
Using the SORTED_DATA keyword reduces the amount of
space required to build a clustered index but SQL Server will then
assume the data **is** sorted. It checks that each row is greater
than the previous and if not the process fails and you get an error

Create clustered indexes before non-clustered indexes
(i.e. it should be the first index created)
because it will sort the data

12.3B Nonclustered Indexes

Rows are NOT maintained in a sorted order
The physical order and the indexed order are NOT the same
The 'leaf' level is in the indexed pages
Each leaf level page contains a pointer to rows on the data pages
    i.e. the leaf level is an extra level between the data and the index

Illustration of Nonclustered Indexed Table

Root level

Key	Page
G	100

Node or non-Leaf level

Page 100

Key	Page
G	6
J	4
H	5

Page 101

Key	Page
X	1
S	5
L	5

Leaf level

Page 1	Page 2	Page 3	Page 4	Page 5	Page 6
Q	J	W	D	S	D
X	Y	F	J	L	W
I	C	O	R	H	G

Example: Find G

Root		=>	Page 100
Node:	Page 100	=>	Page 6
Leaf:	Page 6	=>	Data for key = G

Create clustered indexes before nonclustered indexes

There can up to 249 non-clustered Indexes per table

Each index can provide access to data in a different order

They can be created:
1. explicitly CREATE INDEX statement
2. implicitly with a constraint

Index pages are arranged in a hierarchical tree structure with pointers
from the leaf-level pages to the data pages

There can be multiple nonclustered index per table

Consider using a nonclustered index for:

1. Columns that contain a large number of unique values
   E.G.   a *customer_id* column of a *customer* table

2. Queries that return small or single-row results sets
   E.G.
   SELECT * FROM employee
   WHERE emp_id = 'ABC23459G'

3. Queries that use an ORDER BY clause
   and the FASTFIRSTROW optimizer hint.

The leaf-level pages of a nonclustered index are index pages,
which contain indexed column data and pointers to data pages

The pages that hold the actual data can be unordered in any way
or ordered in a different way to the index
(perhaps ordered/sorted by a clustered index)

When the selectivity of a query (a partial result set) reaches around 5%
of the number of rows in the table it may be less expensive for the
optimizer to use a table scan than to use the nonclustered index

The SQL Server optimizer estimates how many I/Os would be required
for each strategy and chooses the optimal one

12.4 Characteristics of Indexes

12.4A Unique Indexes

A unique index is one that allows no duplicate values

It checks each time data is added with an INSERT or UPDATE

If a duplicate value is found it cancels the transaction and
    returns an error message

Unique indexes are created automatically when
    either:
        - a primary key constraint
        - a unique constraint
    is created

Syntax:

    CREATE UNIQUE INDEX index_name
    ON table_name (column_name)

Example:

    CREATE UNIQUE INDEX title_index
    ON titles (title_no)

Note: This would work if there was such a column as title_no

Unique indexes enforce entity (row) integrity

Uniqueness is also enforced on NULL so if you allow NULL then a unique index will allow only one
    note this when considering composite indexes

You cannot create a unique index on a column that already
    contains duplicates (even if IGNORE_DUP_KEY is set)

12.4B Composite Indexes

Used to search 2 - 16 columns as a unit (16 cols max)

All columns must be in the same table

Maximum length of an index (sum of the column lengths) is 256 bytes

Column order in CREATE INDEX does not have to be
the same as Column Order in the Table definition

Syntax:

    CREATE INDEX index_name
    ON   table_name (col_name, col_name, col_name, etc)

Example

    CREATE INDEX loan_index
    ON   loans (isbn, copy_no)

The index is used only when the **first** column of the composite
key is specified in the WHERE clause
(unless an optimizer hint is provided)

The whole index does not have to be used by a query to be utilized
by the optimizer

An index in a different order is a different index
e.g. col1,col2 <> col2,col1

Use the most unique column first in the composite order

Each index has its own set of data pages - with the same capacity (2K)
as other pages. The number of entries on a page depends upon
the size of the index

A long index will be less efficient than a short index.

12.5 Performance Considerations

12.5A Index Usage

The optimizer has, basically, 2 choices:
- *use an index*
- *scan the table*

A small table will always be table scanned

Indexes that are likely to be used are called useful indexes

Only one index can be used for each table in a query

Selectivity is an estimate of the percentage of the rows that will be returned for a query

The smaller the percentage (i.e. the higher the selectivity) returned the more useful the index

If the first column of a combination index has poor selectivity it may be Ignored by the optimizer, so place highly selective columns first (Usually when selectivity is <5% a table scan will result)

The optimizer can usually be relied upon to choose the most <u>useful</u> index and use that index

If the table is small or the percentage returned is large then a table scan will be performed

A logical I/O operation will result in a physical I/O only when the page is not still in cache This is important to remember when reading the I/O statistics for a query because physical I/O can distort the picture

When no index is available a table scan must read every data page in the table.

When an index is available the optimizer determines whether using that index will result in fewer page I/Os than a table scan by using distribution page statistics Therefore run UPDATE STATISTICS regularly
Note: statistics are calculated on the first column of the index only

The overall strategy should be to:
1. anticipate the type of queries required
2. define useful indexes that will minimize table scans
3. let the optimizer take it from there (including the indexed column name in the WHERE clause will increase the chances of the optimizer using it)

SHOWPLAN

SET SHOWPLAN ON | OFF

SHOWPLAN shows each step in joining tables and which indexes it chose
It can be used to confirm use of a particular index

A clustered index is very useful when a query will return a range of values because the data is arranged in order, as specified in the CREATE TABLE statement

A non-clustered index is very useful when a query returns a small set of data because the index will be searched a limited number of times

The corollary is true, a non-clustered index is not useful if a large proportion of the rows are to be returned. The optimizer will therefore choose to scan the table and traverse the pages it located at the start of the result set

Execution Time

SET STATISTICS TIME ON

will return a report of how long it takes for the:
- Parse and Compile time and
- Execution time

for each query you run

Example:

```
SELECT au_fname
FROM    authors
WHERE   au_fname LIKE "a%"
```

Returns:

SQL Server Parse and Compile Time:"   cpu time = 0 ms.

```
    au_fname              au_lname
    --------------------  --------------------------------------
    Abraham      Bennet
    Ann          Dull
    Akiko        Yokomoto
    Anne         Ringer
    Albert       Ringer
    (5 row(s) affected)
```

"SQL Server Execution Times:" cpu time = 0 ms. elapsed time = 30 ms.
Note: The time is zero because it is a very small table and too short to return a value
>   cpu time < 1 msec

Useful Indexes ET AL

Effective index design is very important in achieving good
> SQL Server performance.

Because indexes are not considered part of the logical database design,
> they can be dropped, added, and changed
> without affecting the schema or the data.

You can experiment with indexes because it will affect only
> performance, not data, in a database.

The SQL Server query optimizer can use an index to reduce
> the number of logical page I/Os required

(The number of logical page I/Os is the best criteria because
> a logical I/O will result in a physical page I/O from the
> hard disk only when the page is not in cache.)

If no index is available, SQL Server must perform a table scan

When an index is available, and the optimizer determines that using
> that index will result in fewer logical page I/Os than a table scan,
> it will use that index.

Indexes that are likely to be used by the optimizer are called *useful indexes*.

This means that you must anticipate the types of queries required and
> define useful indexes to minimize table scans.

The usefulness of an index depends on the selectivity of the data for a query.

Selectivity is an estimate of the percentage of the rows in a table
    that are returned for a query.

The SQL Server optimizer uses distribution statistics
    (which are compiled on the first column in a composite index only)
        - to evaluate available indexes,
        - estimate the number of page I/Os required, and
    chooses the method that will result in the fewest logical page I/Os.

The WHERE clause of queries, is the primary focus of the optimizer.
    since each column included in the WHERE clause is
    a possible candidate for an index.

For optimal performance, consider the following useful indexes for
a given *column_x* in the WHERE clause:
- A single-column index on *column_x*
- A multicolumn index, where *column_x* is the first column of the index

Avoid defining a multicolumn index where *column_x* is the second or later column in the index. This would not be a useful index.

Example: SELECT au_id, au_lname, au_fname
         FROM authors
         WHERE au_lname = 'White'

an index on the following columns could be useful to the optimizer:
- *au_lname*
- *au_lname, au_fname*

but an index on these columns would not be useful to the optimizer:
- *au_address*
- *au_fname, au_lname*

Consider using narrow indexes with one or two columns.

Narrow composite indexes may be more effective than wider indexes.

Narrow indexes have more rows per page and fewer index levels,
    therefore, will increase the efficiency of that index
    (Note: efficiency and effectiveness are not synonymous)

A greater number of narrow indexes provides the optimizer
    with more possibilities to choose from

A lesser number of wide, multicolumn indexes provides the optimizer
    with fewer possibilities to choose from
    but may be more effective

For multicolumn indexes, SQL Server maintains:
    - density statistics (used for joins) on all columns of the index and
    - histogram statistics only on the first column of the index.

Note: if the first column of a compound index has poor selectivity,
    the optimizer may not use the index

Because changes to a table might affect the indexes on that table,
    each index can slow INSERT, UPDATE, and DELETE performance

Therefore:
1. experiment with a new index and examine its effect on performance.
2. avoid a large number of indexes on a single table,
3. avoid overlapping indexes that contain shared columns.

Selectivity

Examine the number of unique data values in a column
    as a proportion of the number of rows in the table

This is the selectivity of that column,
    which can help you decide if a column is a candidate for an index
    and, if so, what type of index.

You can use the following query to return the number of unique
    values for a column:

SELECT COUNT (DISTINCT *column_name*) **FROM** *table_name*

Example return values and the type of index
    to consider putting on *column_name* in a 10,000-row table:

Unique values	Index
5000	Nonclustered index
20	Clustered index
3	No index

Traversing data pages

Once a query has located data via an index, it will traverse the pages
    until the query criteria no longer holds true

Therefore when a clustered index results in the data being in the same
    order as the query is looking for (e.g. searching for ranges)
    a clustered index is most efficient

A non-clustered index is useful when a query returns a small result set
    because the index is interogated only a limited number of times

The corollary is true, if every row (or a large proportion of rows) is to
    be returned then an index will not result in efficient data retreival
    - a table scan will be more efficient

Hot-spots

When a number of rows are being inserted into a table that has
    a clustered index that arranges the data in the same order
        as the INSERT statement is accessing it,
    each inserted row must go at the end of the table

While each row is being inserted into the last data page
    (thus locking the data page),
    all other inserted rows must wait until that insert is completed

To remedy this, the data should be arranged in a different order (by using a clustered index on a different column) arranged so that INSERTs take place throughout the table and not just on the last page

For example, do not put a clustered index on the invoice number in the sales table rather mix the data by using a clustered index on customer_id or some other column that ensures INSERTs to data pages will be scattered over many pages. A non-clustered index could be placed on the Invoice#

Note: this is not a panacea solution and should be tailored to the situation Also modern databases do not suffer from the 'hot-spot' – they can deal with it

Placing Tables/Indexes on separate physical hard drives

To place an index on a separate physical hard drive use **ON segment**
(when the segment is on the appropriate hard drive)
This will result in the table being placed on the defined segment
(and hard drive) since the data forms the leaf level of the index

Example:

```
CREATE INDEX    ind_title_id
ON              titles(title_id)
ON              segment110
```

12.5B Optimizer Hints

The Optimizer hints option in a FROM clause allows:
- *override of the optimizer*
- *fine tuning of index selection*
- *control of explicit locking at the table level*
- *specifying that a particular index or no index (table scan) should be used*

Syntax: in the FROM clause:

FROM table_name (INDEX = index_name|index_id))

Example of using a forced index:

    SELECT au_lname, au_fname, phone
    FROM authors (INDEX = aunmind)
    WHERE au_lname ="Jones"

Example of using a forced table scan:

    SELECT au_lname, au_fname, phone
    FROM authors (INDEX = 0)
    WHERE au_lname ="Jones"

Example of using a forced clustered index:

    SELECT au_lname, au_fname, phone
    FROM authors (INDEX = 1)
    WHERE au_lname ="Jones"

12.5C The UPDATE STATISTICS command

Optimization depends on the distribution statistics of the 1st column values in an index

If they are likely to have changed,
    e.g. by:
        large amount of data changed, added, removed
        or the table has been truncated
then update the statistics by running UPDATE STATISTICS

Syntax:
    UPDATE STATISTICS table_name index_name

Example:
    UPDATE STATISTICS authors au_index

UPDATE STATISTICS runs autoupdate statistics automatically when:
- *an index is created*
- *an index is recreated*

on any table that contains data

Use STATS_DATE system function or the
    DBCC SHOW_STATISTICS option to see
        when that table's statistics were last updated

Examples:

STATS_DATE:

```
SELECT   'Index Name' = i.name,
         'Statistics Date' = STATS_DATE(i.id, i.indid)
FROM     sysobjects o, sysindexes i
WHERE    o.name = 'authors'
AND      o.id = i.id
```

DBCC SHOW_STATISTICS:
    DBCC SHOW_STATISTICS (authors, UPKCL_auidind)

12.5D Query Covering

'Query covering' occurs when a query is completely satisfied by the
index (therefore the data does not have to be queried).

Unless all columns in the SELECT list and all columns in the WHERE
clause are part of the nonclustered index,
SQL Server must first read the index
(requiring one or more logical page I/Os
depending on the depth of the index)
and then read the data page pointed to by the index.
When these extra logical data page I/Os are required,
the total number of page I/Os required to execute the query
can increase dramatically for large results sets.

Each column in the query is 'covered' by a column in the index.

Query covering' can be looked upon as a mechanism for using the leaf
level of a non-clustered index instead of the data itself.

E.G. You can use a nonclustered index on the 'price' column and
calculate the average price from the leaf level of the index without
having to read the data from the table where the row is much longer

A table scan would read every row in the table,
in addition to this extra read time the rows are
much longer to read than an index row.

Example:
Run sp_help sales to see the indexes available for the sales table.
The index UPKCL_sales includes the columns *stor_id, ord_num, title_id.*

/* This is not a covered query */
SELECT stor_id, ord_num, title_id, qty
FROM sales (index = UPKCL_sales)

/* This is a covered query */
**SELECT stor_id, ord_num, title_id
FROM sales (index = UPKCL_sales)**

Note:

On the pubs database the time difference will not be seen as it is a very small table.

It is used here to illustrate the point only. The optimizer hint is used to force the use of the index because on such a small table a table scan would normally be chosen by the optimizer

12.5E FILLFACTOR

The FILLFACTOR is a % specifying how full you want the index and/or data pages to be when the index is created

It refers to Leaf and Non-Leaf Index Pages

This leaves room for expansion of the index because the Fillfactor is not maintained after the index is initially built

Eventually the index table becomes full and must be reset by dropping and rebuilding the index

Maintaining free space will avoid page splits

An adequate fillfactor helps avoid page splitting and the resulting maintenance overhead

Syntax:

CREATE INDEX index_name
ON loan (col_name, col_name, col_name, etc)
WITH FILLFACTOR = %

Example:

CREATE INDEX loan_index
ON loan (isbn, copy_no)
WITH FILLFACTOR = 75

Settings:

%FILLFACTOR	LEAF	NON-LEAF
0	Fills 100%	Leaves no room for index entries
1-99	% used	Leaves room for index entries
100	Full	Full

For read only databases the optimal is 100 = 100%

The **default** FILLFACTOR is configured at the server level with sp_configure

Syntax example:

sp_configure 'fill factor',75

The Fill Factor Default is 0 (which is 100% full)

PADINDEX

The PADINDEX option requires that the index node pages have the same FILLFACTOR as the leaf level index pages

Syntax:

CREATE INDEX index_name
ON loan (col_name, col_name, col_name, etc)
WITH PADINDEX, FILLFACTOR = %

Example

CREATE INDEX loan_index
ON loan (isbn, copy_no)
WITH PADINDEX, FILLFACTOR = 75

Example strategy 1:

If a table is not updated frequently a high fill factor is appropriate because page splitting will only happen infrequently

Example strategy 2:

When a table is large and frequently accessed with INSERTs, consider:

1. remove hot-spots by ensuring the INSERTs are not all in one place by randomizing the key order

2. use a low fill factor to avoid page splitting

3. place the non-clustered indexes on another disk

4. redesign the application to consider the 80/20 rule and split the table into 'current' and 'prior'

5. experiment with PADINDEX (if page splitting of index pages is ocurring)

12.5F SORTED_DATA & SORTED_DATA_REORG

Both eliminate the sort performed when a clustered index is created
The data must already be sorted or the index creation will fail
    (checks that each value is >= the last value)

Increases performance by saving time when creating an index
SORTED_DATA_REORG also physically copies the
    table pages to a new set of pages and compact the rows
    in these new pages

This is a good idea when data has become fragmented

SORTED_DATA_REORG is always slower than SORTED_DATA
    because it has more work to do
        (SORTED_DATA does not copy the data and rebuild the indexes)

Example:
```
CREATE UNIQUE CLUSTERED INDEX index_name
ON table_name (column_name)
WITH SORTED_DATA
```

12.5G   DBCC SHOWCONTIG

Used to determine if the table or index is heavily fragmented
Fragmentation occurs through data modifications (INSERT,
   UPDATE, DELETE)

Fragmentation can be reduced by dropping and recreating a
   clustered index
Recreating a clustered index will 'compact' the data so that
   the fillfactor is once again applicable

Syntax:

DBCC SHOWCONTIG (table_id [, index_id])

To find the index_id of the clustered index in a table use:

```
SELECT      indid
FROM        sysindexes
WHERE       name = 'nc_index_name'
```

Note: where nc_index_name is the name of the index

Example:
DBCC SHOWCONTIG(496004798)
(to obtain the table ID use SELECT * FROM sysobjects)

Results:
DBCC SHOWCONTIG scanning 'roysched' table...
[SHOW_CONTIG   SCAN ANALYSIS]

Table: 'roysched' (496004798) Indid:	0 dbid:4
TABLE level scan performed.	
Pages Scanned :2	
Extent Switches : 0	
. Pages per Extent : 2.0	
Scan Density [Best Count:Actual Count]	: 100.00% [0:1]
Avg. Bytes free per page	: 724.0
. Page density (full)	: 64.05%
Avg. Bytes free per Overflow page	: 1444.0
Avg. Overflow Page density	: 28.3%
Disconnected Overflow Pages	: 0

DBCC execution completed.

Interpretation:
Pages Scanned No of pages in the table
Extent Switches Number of times the DBCC statement left the extent
Avg. Pages per Extent   No of pages per extent in the page chain
Scan Density [Best Count:Actual Count]   100 = contiguous
Avg. Bytes free per page   Higher is better
Avg. Page density (full) Higher is better

Also use Enterprise Manager\Manage\Indexes to display a GUI to tables and Indexes

Chapter 13 – Scripts and Transactions (incl LOCKS)

You may ask what scripts have to do with transactions. The answer is simple, we are going to look at what SQL Server treats as a complete process

Scripts
A script is a mini-program that is run on the server. One of the reasons you might run a script instead of doing things via the GUI is that you then can make both a hardcopy of what was done and save it electronically for future reference.

For example, setting configuration options can be done with the GUI but what happens if you have a crash and want to reconstruct the database. Model database is a good place to start but it does not reflect the options you have subsequently chosen.

There is a very handy feature in SQL Server call Script Generator which enables you to generate a script and print it out. This follows the philosophy that hardcopy is the ultimate backup. While it is all very well to try to create the paperless office there will always be a place for hardcopy. Hardcopy can be printed and put in an updated file. This can easily be inspected by managers etc that would not gain the same awareness and comfort from a flash drive with the same information on it. However you can also save them to files to have an electronic copy

A script can be in electronic form and electronic copy is just as effective and easier to create, maintain and use, provided you are organized enough to maintain version control and structure in your storage

Transactions
Locks are required to ensure the integrity of transactions so they are dealt with here.
The concept of a transaction as an atomic unit of work and recovery is covered.

Chapter 13:

Scripts and Transactions (incl. Locks)

This module is designed to enable you to:
1. Describe Batches & Scripts
2. Describe Transaction Management
3. Identify the Types of Locks and Locking Levels

Outline - The Context Tool

1 Batches and Scripts		5
1A Scripts		5
1B Batches		6
1C Combining Statements in a single batch		7
1D Batch Rules		7
1E Example of Invalid Batches		8
2 Transaction Management		9
2A Processing		9
2B Database Consistency and Concurrency		9
2C Locks		10
2C.1 Types of Lock		10
2C.1a Shared Locks		10
2C.1b Update Locks		10
2C.1c Exclusive Locks		10
2C.2 What can be locked by SQL Server		11
2C.3 Lock Escalation		12
2C.4 Locking Options		13
2C.4a Row Level Locking		14
2D Transactions		15
2D.1 Transaction is a Unit of Work and a Unit of Recovery		15
2D.2 User-defined transactions		15
2D.3 Rollback		17
2D.4 Savepoint		18

13.1 Batches and Scripts

The relationship between batches and a script

```
                              SELECT
             Batch            UPDATE
                              GO
                              BEGIN TRANS
                              x
Script       Batch            x
                              x
                              COMMIT TRANS
                              GO
             Batch            x
                              x
                              GO
```

13.1A Scripts

A Script is a series of batches submitted one after the other
If one batch within the script fails it is left to the decision of the
      client program whether the other batches are submitted

13.1B Batches

A batch is a set of SQL statements:
- submitted together
- executed as a group

A batch is compiled as a whole
It is terminated with a marker "GO" on a line by itself
Restrictions on batch size:
    an overall limit (including data and execution plan) of 128k
        applies therefore less than 128k of data can be included
the limit does not apply to:
    text or image data
    updates with WRITETEXT or UPDATETEXT
    data inserted with bcp
    data inserted from another table
    data passed by RPCs
Batches can be submitted through :

- *the graphical tool   isql/w*
- *a command line utility isql*
- *scripts (files) passed to isql*

13.1C   Combining Statements in a single batch

The following cannot be combined with other statements in a single batch
    CREATE DEFAULT
    CREATE PROCEDURE
    CREATE RULE
    CREATE TRIGGER
    CREATE VIEW
instead they have to be submitted one at a time

Multiple Statements
    SELECT COUNT(*) FROM titles
    SELECT COUNT(*) FROM authors
2 result sets will be returned

You can combine: CREATE DATABASE . . .
                    CREATE TABLE . . . .
                    CREATE INDEX
                    GO

but not   CREATE DATABASE . . .
                    CREATE TABLE . . . .
                    CREATE RULE
                    CREATE RULE
                    GO

instead you should: CREATE DATABASE . . .
                    GO
                    CREATE TABLE . . . .
                    GO
                    CREATE RULE
                    GO
                    CREATE RULE
                    GO

13.1D Batch Rules

Rules and Defaults cannot be Bound to Columns and used
    in the same batch
        i.e. sp_bindrule and sp_bindefault cannot be used in the same
            batch as INSERT and UPDATE that invoke the rule or default
       * CHECK constraints cannot be defined and used in the same batch

You cannot DROP an Object and Recreate it in the same batch
        e.g.   DROP TABLE table
                  CREATE TABLE table
                SELECT * FROM table

Options changed with SET statement take effect at the End of the batch
        i.e. While you can use SET statements and queries in the same
            batch but the SET option will not apply to that batch

    • You cannot alter a table and then reference the new columns inthe same batch

13.1E Invalid Batch Examples

EG.1
```
CREATE VIEW testview
AS
SELECT column1        Valid
FROM test
GO
```

EG.2 EG.2
```
USE PUBS
SELECT *              Valid
FROM authors
GO
```

EG.3
```
CREATE VIEW testview
AS        SELECT column1    Cannot combine CREATE VIEW
FROM test
INSERT testview
VALUES ('Hello')
GO
```

EG.4
```
DROP VIEW test           Cannot combine DROP VIEW
CREATE VIEW test
        (column1 char(12), column2 int)
GO
```

EG.5
```
CREATE TABLE test
        (column1 char(10)
        CONSTRAINT CK_c1 CHECK (column1 = 'Quack')
        column2 int)         Cannot combine CONSTRAINT

INSERT test
VALUES ('Woof, 598')

SELECT *
FROM test
GO
```

13.2 Transaction Management

A transaction is a single unit of work
Any single SQL statement is considered a single unit of work
    whether it affects 1 or more rows within a table
In SQL Server a transaction is:
    implicit - due to the nature of the statements executed
    explicit - as defined by the user
All explicit transaction must be enclosed within:
    BEGIN TRAN
    COMMIT TRAN
Transactions apply to data modification statements only
Grouping a large number of T SQL statements into one
    long running transaction can increase recovery time
    and cause concurrency problems
It is best if the COMMIT statement is in the same batch as the BEGIN statement

13.2A Processing - ATOMICITY

Transaction processing guarantees database consistency
    and recoverability by:
- *either the entire transaction is completed and all changes are made in the database*
- *or the transaction is rolled back*

13.2B Database Consistency and Concurrency

When more than one user accesses a database concurrently
   then a method is needed to ensure that they do not
   interfere with each other and data remains consistent
SQL Server uses locking techniques to achieve its goal
Locks are held on data that is being read or modified during
   a transaction to prevent problems that could arise from multiple access
Locking can be applied in various ways (and each has its own
   characteristics) but keep in mind that locks should be
   minimized to increase performance
The objectives of locking are to prevent a transaction from:
- modifying pages that being read by another transaction
- modifying pages that being modified by another transaction
- reading pages that being modified by another transaction

13.2C Locks

13.2C.1 Types of Lock

SQL Server uses 3 types of locks to maintain data consistency
1. Shared
2. Update Locks
3. Exclusive

13.2C.1a Shared Locks

Used for operations that do not change data (e.g. SELECT)
   i.e. read only operations
They are used at the Page level or the Table level

More than 1 transaction can apply shared locks
   i.e. there can be >1 lock on the data

They are released after the transaction is done
   but the data is not free until the last transaction releases it

13.2C.1b Update Locks

Used when data is <u>to be</u> modified and promoted to 'exclusive'
   before actual modification

They are used at the Page level only

Are applied when the pages are being read
    e.g. during the initial stage of an update

Are compatible with shared locks,
    therefore you can lock more than one to a page

Are promoted to 'exclusive' locks before pages are changed

Only one UPDATE lock can be obtained on a resource
    (page, extent or table)
    If another UPDATE lock is requested it has to wait

13.2C.1c   Exclusive Locks

Used for data modifications (Write operations)
    i.e. INSERT, UPDATE, DELETE
They are used at the Page level or the Table level
Are applied by only one transaction at a time
No transaction can acquire an exclusive lock or another update lock
    until all shared locks have been released

Resolving Locks conflicts

Conflicts are resolved by SQL Server assigning priorities
    to processes. With an update lock in place
    no further locks can be placed on the page and
    SQL Server will wait until all SHARED locks are released
    before upgrading the UPDATE lock to an EXCLUSIVE lock

13.2C.2 What can be locked by SQL Server

The following can be the subject of locks:

1. Page - a 2K Data Page or an Index Page
   This is the most common type

2. Extent - a contiguous group of 8 Data or Index Pages
   This is used only while they are allocated or freed
   Extent locks are set while a CREATE or DROP statement is running or while an INSERT statement that requires new data or index pages is running.

3. An entire Table (including both data and indexes)

4. Intent - a special type of table lock which indicates the type of page locks currently on the table

Compatibility between lock types

While a lock is held on a specific Page only compatible locks can be placed on that Page

	Shared	Update	Exclusive
Shared	Comp	Comp	Incomp
Update	Comp	Incomp	Incomp
Exclusive	Incomp	Incomp	Incomp

Note: that an UPDATE lock is incompatible with another UPDATE lock

13.2C.3   Lock Escalation

SQL Server implements locking automatically
   but the systems administrator can customize locking by:
   1   using SELECT statement options
   2   choosing an isolation level with the SET statement
   3   setting the lock escalation level which determines when page locks escalate to table locks

Escalation thresholds

A query requests rows and, usually, page level locks are generated
   but if the query requests a large proportion of the rows then locking is escalated to table level

Lock escalation makes table scans and operations more efficient
   because it reduces locking overhead

Lock escalation options apply per statement (not per transaction)

Escalation threshold is set at the Server level with sp_configure
   It cannot be over ridden

Options that can be set
1   LE Threshold Maximum   (LE = Lock Threshold)
   Maximum number of page locks before escalation
   Default = 200
   Escalation occurs despite the LE Percentage

2   LE Threshold Minimum
   Minimum number of page locks before escalation
   Default = 20
   Prevents escalation for small tables
   Escalation only occurs once both the LE Percentage and the minimum is exceeded

3   LE Threshold Percentage
   Specifies the percentage of Page locks on a table before a table lock is requested
   Default = 0

13.2C.4 Locking Options

You can specify one or more locking options in a SELECT statement

NOLOCK
    The 'Dirty Read' option
    directs SQL Server not to issue shared locks
        nor honor exclusive locks
    It is then possible to read non-committed transactions
        or a set of pages that are rolled back in the middle of a read

HOLDLOCK
    Instructs SQL Server to hold a shared lock until completion
        of the transaction in which HOLDLOCK is issued
        instead of releasing the lock as soon as no longer needed

UPDLOCK
    directs SQL Server to use update locks instead of
        shared locks while reading a table and hold it until
        completion of the transaction
    UPDLOCK allows data reads (including other readers) and
    update it later (without the data changing in the meantime)

TABLOCK
    directs SQL Server to use a shared lock on a table
    allows others to read the table but not update it
    lock is held until the end of the command
        unless HOLDLOCK is also specified

PAGLOCK
    directs SQL Server to use page locking (the default)

TABLOCKX
    directs SQL Server to use an Exclusive lock on a table
        prevents others from reading or updating
        is held until the end of the transaction

These locking options override session level options set with
    the SET statement

Transaction Isolation Level

When you set the Isolation Level using SET ISOLATION LEVEL
you specify the default locking behavior for all SELECT statements in the SQL Server session

It can be overridden in individual SELECT statements

Use DBCC USEROPTIONS to return what isolation level is set

Isolation level options

READ COMMITTED
directs SQL Server to use shared locks while reading
- you cannot experience 'dirty reads'

READ UNCOMMITTED
directs SQL Server not to issue shared locks and does not honor exclusive locks
you can experience 'dirty reads' and can get phantom values from rollback because of reading uncommitted transactions
(after a rollback the value you read did not exist)

REPEATABLE READ or SERIALIZABLE (they're interchangeable)
indicates that 'dirty read' non-repeatable reads
phantom errors cannot occur

13.2C.4a Row Level Locking

Areas of unusually high access are called Hotspots.'

When concurrent users attempt to insert data into the table's
  last page and compete for exclusive use a hotspot develops

The situation might be improved with row-level locking

By default the locking level of SQL Server is a page
  which can contain 'x' rows

While there is no real substitute for a well designed application
  there are specific situations where IRL (INSERT Row-level
  Locking) is useful

The most common situation is where hotspots are ocurring on
  tables which are structured as sequential files and
  records are inserted at the end of the table

A hotspot often ocurrs if:
  1   the table has no index
  2   the table has a non-clustered index
  3   the table has a clustered index with an increasing key
       (e.g. an INDENTITY column)

Syntax:
  exec sp_tableoption 'tablename', insert row lock', true

13.2D Transactions

13.2D.1 A Transaction is a Unit of Work and a Unit of Recovery

Because all transactions are recorded in a write ahead log
    SQL Server databases can be recovered after:
1. power loss
2. system software failure
3. application problems
4. transaction cancellation requests

This transaction log is key to transaction processing

When a request to modify the data is received:
    the changes are first recorded in the log
    then the old data is recorded in the log
    then the new data is written to the database
The process of recording changes in the log before the
    data is updated is known as **write ahead**

During recovery incomplete transactions are backed out of the
    log to restore the database to its previous state
    This is called rolling back the transactions

The log is also used to ensure that all committed transactions
    are fully reflected in the database

13.2D.2 User defined Transactions

User defined transactions (explicit transactions)
> give the user control of transaction management

Users can group sets of SQL statements into a Transaction

A group of statements requires:
> BEGIN TRAN (tran_name)
>> SQL Statement
>> SQL Statement
>
> COMMIT TRAN (tran_name)

but not a single statement

Example:

To change the royalty percentages between the 2 authors of one book
> changes have to be made to two rows in the titleauthor table
> In order to prevent any chance of an inconsistency
> (the percentages totaling >100%) a transaction may be
> written that contains both UPDATE statements

```
BEGIN TRAN
    UPDATE titleauthor
        SET royaltyper = 65
        FROM titleauthor, titles
        WHERE royaltyper = 75
        AND titleauthor.title_id = titles.title_id
        AND title = "The Gourmet Cookbook"
    UPDATE titleauthor
        SET royaltyper = 35
        FROM titleauthor, titles
        WHERE royaltyper = 25
        AND titleauthor.title_id = titles.title_id
        AND title = "The Gourmet Cookbook"
COMMIT TRAN
```

Rules:

Transaction names must conform to the rules of identifiers
No special permissions are needed to define a transaction

Temporary tables cannot be created from inside a transaction
     therefore some systems procedures cannot be used
     because they create temporary tables

The following statements cannot be used in a transaction:

> all DROP statements
> DISK INIT
> CREATE DATABASE
> ALTER DATABASE
> CREATE TABLE
> ALTER TABLE
> TRUNCATE TABLE
> SELECT INTO (because it creates a table)
> LOAD DATABASE
> LOAD TRANSACTION
> DUMP TRANSACTION
> CREATE VIEW
> CREATE INDEX
> CREATE PROCEDURE
> GRANT/REVOKE PERMISSION
> RECONFIGURE
> UPDATE STATISTICS

13.2D.3   Rollback Transaction

Syntax:
> ROLLBACK TRAN [tran_name | savepoint_name]

A transaction or only a part of a transaction can be rolled back
> at any time before a commit transaction but not after

Transactions can be nested (can call each other)
> but only the outermost transaction is registered with the system
> and a rollback call to any inner transaction generates an error

No portion of a transaction is committed until the outer COMMIT
> TRAN is issued

Apparent transaction nesting occurs when a trigger or stored
> procedure (containing a transaction) calls each other
>> @@TRANCOUNT is used to determine if there are any open transactions (and how deep they are nested)

When @@TRANCOUNT = 0 there are no open transactions

BEGIN TRAN increments @@TRANCOUNT and

ROLLBACK TRAN decrements @@TRANCOUNT

13.2D.4   SAVEPOINT

Syntax:
SAVE TRAN savepoint_name

A SAVEPOINT is a marker that indicates a point in a transaction to which it can be rolled back (in addition to BEGIN TRAN)
SAVEPOINTs are inserted by placing a SAVE TRANSACTION in a transaction

Example:

To include another set of SQL statements that you only wish to use on a temporary basis you could insert a SAVE TRAN after the SQL statements in the previous example and roll back to that point

```
BEGIN TRAN
    UPDATE titleauthor
        SET royaltyper = 65
        FROM titleauthor, titles
        WHERE royaltyper = 75
        AND titleauthor.title_id = titles.title_id
        AND title = "The Gourmet Cookbook"
    UPDATE titleauthor
        SET royaltyper = 35
        FROM titleauthor, titles
        WHERE royaltyper = 25
        AND titleauthor.title_id = titles.title_id
        AND title = "The Gourmet Cookbook"

    SAVE TRAN percentage_changed

    UPDATE titles
        SET price = price * 1.1
        WHERE title = "The Gourmet Cookbook"
    SELECT (price * royalty * ytd_sales) * royaltyper
        FROM titleauthor, titles
        WHERE title = "The Gourmet Cookbook"
        AND titleauthor.title_id = titles.title_id
    ROLLBACK TRAN percentage_changed

COMMIT TRAN
```
Note: you would normally do something with the result of the SELECT query

CHAPTER 14:

PROGRAMMING

This module should probably be entitled 'Control-of-Flow language and Cursors' for that is what it contains. The term 'Programming' is far too wide in the scope of the term. However, this chapter addresses some of the issues that SQL Server developers will use while writing the scripts we discussed in the last chapter and the content surely fits within the term 'Programming.'

Control-of Flow language
Whether you learned programming in COBOL, Fortran, Pascal, P/L1, C# or Basic you are familiar with the basic contructs and techniques of programming. This book is not intended to teach programming nor the techniques of error handling, control break structures, nesting or loops. Some of the available programming features are introduced and merely introduced. It is hoped that Programmers will forgive and non-programmers explore further with other educational sources. This text is an introduction and a discussion of the available Control-of-Flow commands only.

Cursors
The second part of the chapter discusses cursors and introduces the concept of row by row processing. Readers should note that this is not what SQL Server was designed for. Set theory, on which the T-SQL language is based, deals with resultsets and not with each and every row. Nevertheless there is definitely a need for cursors and therefore an understanding of how they work is essential.

Chapter 14 - Programming

This module is designed to enable you to:
1. Identify Control-of-Flow statements
2. Use Cursors to work through a ResultSet
3. Use CASE in SELECT, UPDATE, DELETE
4. Describe the benefits of the EXECUTE statement
5. Dynamically build a Transact-SQL statement using EXEC

Outline - The Context Tool

14.1 Control of Flow Language — 5
14.1A DECLARE — 5
　　14.1A.1 Local variables — 6
　　14.1A.2 Global variables — 7
14.1B RETURN — 10
14.1C RAISERROR — 10
14.1D PRINT — 12
14.1E CASE — 13
14.1F BEGIN . . . END Block — 15
14.1G IF . . . ELSE Block — 15
14.1H WHILE construct — 16
14.1I EXECUTE — 17
14.1J WAIT FOR DELAY — 19

14.2 Cursors — 20
14.2A ANSI Cursors — 20
14.2B Enhanced Engine Cursors — 20
14.2C ANSI SQL Cursors — 21
　　14.2C.1 DECLARE statement — 22
　　14.2C.2 OPEN statement — 23
　　14.2C.3 FETCH statement — 24
　　14.2C.4 CLOSE statement — 24
　　14.2C.5 DEALLOCATE statement — 25
14.2D When to use Cursors — 25

14.1 Control of Program Flow Language

14.1A DECLARE

Variables are defined with DECLARE

Without Control of Flow language SQL statements would be executed sequentially

Control of Flow language enables statements to be:
- *connected*
- *related*
- *made interdependent*

using programming like constructs

Control of Flow keywords

DECLARE
RETURN
RAISERROR
PRINT
CASE
BEGIN . . . END
IF . . . ELSE
WHILE
BREAK . . . CONTINUE

14.1A.1   Local Variables

Local variable start with a single @, global variable start with @@

A value can be assigned to the variable with a SELECT only
    after it has been declared

Syntax:
    DECLARE @variable_name datatype [,@variable_name datatype, etc]

Example:
```
DECLARE    @next char(25)
SELECT  @next = " "
WHILE      @next is not null
BEGIN
        SELECT  @next = min(name)
        FROM    sysobjects
        WHERE   type = "U"
        AND        name > @next
        EXEC       sp_spaceused @next
END
```

The batch executes sp_spaceused for each table in the database
Because it can execute on only one table at a time the batch
must declare a variable (called @next) into which it can
    save the table name.
The min(name) function gets the lowest value of name that has not
    already been processed.
The AND name > @next clause passes execution to the next
    alphabetically highest tablename until @next reaches the NULL
    state at the end

Variables can be used as parameters in (for example):
    EXECUTE
    RAISERROR
    PRINT

14.1A.2 Global Variables

Global variables are pre defined and maintained by the system
They are prefixed by the @@ symbols

Many global variables report on system activity since the
last time the server was started:

@@CONNECTIONS	Number of logon attempts
@@CPU_BUSY	Amount of CPU time on SQL Server work since SQL Server was started
@@IDLE	Amount of idle time since SQL Server was started
@@IO_BUSY	Amount of time spent on Input & Output operations
@@PACK_RECEIVED	Number of input packets received
@@PACK_SENT	Number of input packets sent
@@PACKET_ERRORS	Number of errors that occurred while SQL Server was sending/receiving packets
@@TOTAL_ERRORS	Number of errors that occurred since SQL Server was started
@@TOTAL_READ	Number of Disk reads
@@TOTAL_WRITE	Number of Disk writes

Other global variables report on information about the server:

@@DBTS	Timestamp datatype
@@LANGID	ID of the Current language
@@LANGUAGE	Current language
@@MAX_CONNECTIONS	Max number of connections allowed
@@MAX_PRECISION	Level of precision set
@@SERVERNAME	Name of the Server
@@SERVICENAME	Name of the Service that is running
@@TIMETICKS	Number of microseconds per tick
@@TEXTSIZE	Number of bytes of text or image a SELECT returns
@@VERSION	Date and current Version number of SQL Server

14.1B RETURN

Exits unconditionally from a query or a procedure
    statements following the RETURN are not executed
Stored procedures can return an integer value to:
- *the calling procedure*
- *the application*

Syntax: RETURN [integer]

Example:
```
CREATE PROC checkmem @param int
AS
IF (SELECT   member_no
      FROM  loan
      WHERE      member_no = @param) <= 4
    RETURN 1
ELSE
    RETURN 2
```

User defined status values should not conflict with SQL Server

SQL Server reserves: 0 = successful
    1 to 99 to indicate different reasons for failure
       of which only 1 to 14 are currently reserved
    (-1 means the Object is missing
    - 2 means a Datatype error has occurred)

To capture a returned value you have to execute your stored
    procedure in a specific format:

Syntax:
    EXEC   @returned_status_variable = procedure_name

Example:
```
DECLARE    @status int
EXEC       @status = delete_member
WHILE      @status = 0
    BEGIN
        PRINT "Query successful"
        BREAK
    END
```

14.1C RAISERROR

While SQL Server will handle most error reporting for you,
- transmitting a message and identifying the problem, the RAISERROR command enables user defined error messages

Returning an error condition with an identifier is particularly
- useful when using batches, stored procedures or triggers

RAISERROR returns a user defined error message and
- sets a system flag to record that an error has been recorded

RAISERROR can record a message to the WinNT event log or
- in the SQL Server log

RAISERROR lets the client application:
- retrieve an error message from the sysmessages table
- or
- build a message dynamically with:
  - user_specified severity and
  - state information

After definition the message is sent back to the client application
- as a server error message

All ad hoc messages have one standard message ID of 50000

Syntax:

RAISERROR msg_id | msg_string, severity, state
  (arguement1, arguement2)
WITH LOG

The WITH LOG option writes the error to both the SQL Server
- error log and the WinNT event log

Example 1:

RAISERROR ("Invalid ID", 16, 1)

Example 2:

RAISERROR ("Done", 1, 1)

Example 3:

RAISERROR ('The level for job_id: %d should be between %d and %d.',
   16,   -- severity level
   -1,   -- state
   @job_id,   -- arguement 1
   @min_lvl,   -- arguement 2
   @max_lvl)   -- arguement 3

The 3 arguements will be substituted for the variables (%d) defined in the message

Note: see the script "instpubs" for the way Microsoft builds messages

The WITH LOG option is required for a severity level
  of 19 through 25 (which defined a SQL Server event)
  and can only be issued by the systems administrator

Error messages consist of 4 elements:

1 Error number:
  A unique integer between 50,001 and (2^{31} -1)
  Client applications will trap certain errors but pass others
   through to the user
    e.g. Deadlocks are usually handled internally
  A duplicate key in a table may be reported to the user
  An **sa** may be alerted when the database log is full

2 Severity
  level 1 to 10 are informational
  levels 11-16 are error conditions that the user can typically correct
  levels 17 to 19 indicate a software or hardware problem
  levels 20 to 25 indicate system problems (usually system fatal)

3 State

   An integer value 1 - 127

4   Message

The text (not to exceed 255 characters)

To generate a SQL Server error programmatically use the RAISERROR command to place the error number you specify in the @@error global variable and transmit:
- *the error number*
- *the severity assigned to it*
- *the state*
- *the message to the client application*

SQL Server provides a number of internal error messages related to pre-defined events

These error messages are stored in a system table sysmessages

You can add your own messages to sysmessages and refer to them in a RAISERROR statement using numbers from 50,001 to 2^{31}

Ad hoc error messages always use number 50,000

You can write an ad hoc message by providing the text of the message instead of the error number

Example of an ad hoc error message:

> **RAISERROR ("Invalid ID", 15,1)**
> **Msg 50000, level 15, state 1, Invalid ID**

Use **sp_addmessage** to add a message to the sysmessages table

14.1D PRINT

The PRINT statement returns a user defined error message to the client application's message handler

Syntax:

PRINT {Any ASCII text | variable }

Example:

PRINT 'Total = '
PRINT @total
Results (if you had declared and calculated a value for @total):
Total =
30

The message can have up to 255 characters

Variable can be local or global but must be either datatype **char** or datatype **var**

A "formatted" message of more then 1 parameter can be built by using concatenation and building a string

E.G.   **DECLARE   @message varchar(35)**

         SELECT   @message = "Hello " + user_name()
         PRINT   @message

Results: Hello sa

14.1E CASE

The CASE expression allows conditional branching

The Case expression is ANSI compliant and allowed anywhere an expression can be used

Case expressions can be either:

    1   Simple CASE
    2   Searched CASE

Simple CASE expression

Within a SELECT statement the simple CASE expression allows only the equality check

Example:

The CASE expression can be used to make the description more readable

```
SELECT Category = CASE type
        WHEN 'popular_comp' THEN 'Popular Computing'
        WHEN 'mod cook' THEN 'Modern Cooking'
        WHEN 'business' THEN 'Business'
        etc
        END
```

Searched CASE expression

The following selection covers all the possibilities because of the ELSE

Example:

```
SELECT "Price Category" =
    CASE    WHEN price IS NULL THEN "Not yet priced"
            WHEN price < 10 THEN "Very Reasonable"
            WHEN price >= 10 and price <20
                THEN "Coffee Table Title"
            ELSE "Expensive"
    END,
    "Shortened Title" = CONVERT(varchar(20), title),
    Category = CASE type
            WHEN "popular_comp"
                THEN "Popular Computing"
            WHEN "mod_cook" THEN "Modern Cooking"
```

```
                    WHEN "business" THEN "Business"
                    WHEN "trad_cook" THEN "Traditional Cooking"
                    WHEN "psychology" THEN "Psychology"
                    ELSE "Undecided"
                    END
            FROM titles
            ORDER BY price
```

Results:

Price Category	Shortened Title	Category
Not yet priced	Net Etiquette	Popular Computing etc

See p21 of the Transact SQL Reference for an example of an UPDATE statement used with a CASE expression

The searched CASE expression allows the full use of boolean logic and AND and OR between expressions

Example 1: (excert)

```
'Sales are ' +
    CASE
            WHEN ytd_sales < 5000 then 'poor'
            WHEN ytd_sales BETWEEN 5000 AND 10000 then 'OK'
            WHEN ytd_sales > 10000 then 'great'
        ELSE "Sales unknown"
    END
```

ELSE expression

The ELSE expression is optional and covers all situations not covered by the WHEN statements

If there is no ELSE option a NULL is returned when all the WHEN clauses fail

Example 2:

A case statement can be used to produce a cross-tab report.
Examples include:
- 1   an accounts receivable aging
- 2   a debit column, credit column report

COALESCE - Searched CASE equivalent

COALESCE (expr1, expr2)
is equivalent to a searched CASE expression
where a NOT NULL *expression1* returns *expression1*
and a NULL *expression1* returns *expression2*
In searched CASE expression form, it would look like this:

```
CASE WHEN expression1 IS NOT NULL
    THEN expression1
        ELSE expression2
END
```

Example (run these in the pubs database):
```
SELECT * FROM discounts

UPDATE discounts
SET highqty = 99
WHERE discounttype = "Customer Discount"

SELECT * FROM discounts

SELECT COALESCE(lowqty, highqty) FROM discounts
```

Note: Coalesce returned the first non-NULL from the list (lowqty, highqty)

14.1F BEGIN . . . . END Block

Marks the beginning and end of an group of SQL statements that you wish to be treated an indivisible a block

Example:

```
IF EXISTS    (SELECT * FROM authors
             WHERE au_lname = "Smith")
BEGIN
    PRINT "Smith exists"
    EXEC sproc_found
END
ELSE
BEGIN
    PRINT "Smith does not exist"
    EXEC sproc_notfound
END
```

Although it can be used anywhere BEGIN . . . END commonly used in IF . . ELSE and WHILE

BEGIN . . . END blocks can be nested

14.1G   IF . . . . ELSE Block

Allows a condition to be imposed upon the execution of a statement

The statement is Boolean in nature

  i.e. IF {condition is true} contents of { } are implied
        SQL statement or block
ELSE {condition is false}
        SQL statement or block

IF . . ELSE constructs can be used in Batches, Stored Procedures
       and ad hoc Queries

ELSE is optional

An IF can only execute a single SQL statement unless a
       block is defined with BEGIN . . END

Nesting has a limit of 150 levels which is practically equivalent to
       unlimited providing there is enough stack space

A nested IF is equivalent to an AND operator and the ELSE
       is equivalent to an OR

The CASE statement may be an alternative

if exists is useful for checking referential integrity
       it stops at the first instance of the search match, therefore is
       faster than the count(*) > 0 technique

When used in an IF, SELECT statements must be enclosed in parens

14.1H   WHILE construct

Sets a condition for repeated execution of a SQL statement of block
    for as long as the condition remains true

Execution is controlled within the loop by BREAK and CONTINUE

BREAK causes an exit from the loop

CONTINUE causes the loop to restart - skipping the SQL statements
    after the CONTINUE command

BREAK and CONTINUE are often activated by an IF test

If WHILE loops are nested the inner BREAK exits to the next outer
    level of the nest after running the statements at the end of the
    inner loop

Example:
    If you wanted to raise prices so that the average price is
        less than $30 and the maximum price is less than $50

```
WHILE (SELECT AVG(price) FROM titles) < $30
BEGIN
    UPDATE titles
    SET price = price * 1.1
    SELECT MAX(price) FROM titles
       IF (SELECT MAX(price) FROM titles) > $50
          BREAK
       ELSE
          CONTINUE
END
PRINT 'Prices are now as much as the market will bear'
```

The loop raises the prices until the conditions are met and prints
    the message at the end

Remember this is just an example to illustrate the concepts
    you would not use table scans like this in practice if the tables are
        not small

14.1I   EXECUTE

The EXECUTE statement executes:
1. a system stored procedure
2. a user defined stored procedure
3. an extended stored procedure
4. a character string within a T-SQL batch with variables which can be resolved at execution time

Item 4 above needs further explanation
    All items within the EXEC string must consist of character data
        (I.e. all numerics must be converted prior to building the string, also functions cannot be used)
    However, ANY valid SQL statements (including functions) are available to be passed within the string.

Nested EXEC statements are permitted

Syntax:
    EXEC stored procedure | character string parameter, parameter, . .etc

Examples:

1. **A system stored procedure:**

    EXEC sp_help

    and with a passed parameter

    EXEC sp_help authors

    if this is the 1st statement in a batch or in an isql script, EXEC is not required

2. **A user-defined stored procedure:**

    EXECute procedure_name parameter_name

    Example:

    EXEC roy_check 'PS3333'

3. **A user defined stored procedure with multiple Parameters and an Output Parameter**

    This example executes the **roy_check** stored procedure,

It passes three parameters
The 3rd parameter (@@*pc*), is an OUTPUT parameter.
Once the procedure has executed, the return value is available in the variable @*percent*.

> **DECLARE @percent int**
> **EXECUTE roy_check 'BU1032', 1050, @@pc = @percent OUTPUT**
> **SELECT Percent = @percent**

4   With an Extended Stored Procedure

This example uses the **xp_cmdshell** extended stored procedure to list a directory of all files ending in EXE:

> **EXECUTE xp_cmdshell "dir *.exe"**

5   EXECUTE '*tsql_string*' with a Variable

This example shows how EXECUTE handles dynamically built strings with variables instead of hardcoding the values

> **DECLARE @tablename char(40)**
> **SELECT @tablename = 'titles'**
> **EXEC ('SELECT * FROM ' + @tablename)**

Note: Functions cannot be used to build the string itself
e.g.©
The following are **NOT** permissible:
    EXEC(' SELECT * FROM ' + RTRIM(@table_name))
You also cannot call .exe files from within an execute statement
    EXEC(winword.exe)

6   With a Stored Procedure Variable

This example creates a variable that represents a stored procedure name

> **DECLARE   @proc_name varchar(30)**
> **SELECT   @proc_name = 'sp_who'**
> **EXEC   @proc_name**

7   Complex combination of character strings and variables:

The EXEC statement can include:

- *string variable*
- *string local variable*
- *concatenation of string literals and string local variables*

Syntax: EXEC @str_var|tsql_string + @str_var|tsql_string . . . .

Example:
Create a stored procedure that issues an EXEC statement which will update the statistics on all the user defined tables in a database

```
CREATE PROC sproc_DB_Stats
AS
SET NOCOUNT ON
SELECT        '*** Database: ' + db_name() + ' *** '
DECLARE  @next char(30)
SELECT        @next = ' '
WHILE     @next IS NOT NULL
  BEGIN
    SELECT    sysobjects
    WHERE     type ='U'
    AND       name > @next
    IF        @next IS NOT NULL
    BEGIN
      EXEC ('UPDATE STATISTICS' + @next)
    END
  END
```

14.1J   WAIT FOR

Specifies:
- a time
- time interval
- event

that triggers execution of a:
- statement block
- stored procedure
- transaction

Syntax

WAITFOR DELAY '*time*'

Instructs SQL Server to wait until the specified amount of time has passed (maximum 24 hours)

Example:

WAITFOR DELAY '*00:02:00*'

Syntax

WAITFOR TIME '*time*'

Instructs SQL Server to wait until the specified time

Example:

WAITFOR TIME '*00:02:00*'

The time must be in one of the acceptable formats for *datetime* data

The time you specify can include hours, minutes, and seconds

Use the format '*hh:mm:ss*'

You cannot specify dates

You can also specify a local variable in place of the '*time*' string

14.2   Cursors

Cursors allow individual row operations to be performed on
    a given ResultSet
Conceptually Cursors obtain a ResultSet returned from a database
This can be either, data, or information from the system
    e.g. all the user defined table names
After the cursor has been opened a user can scroll through the
    ResultSet using an operation called FETCH which will interact
    with the underlying data in a manner defined in the cursor

A ResultSet can be e.g. the set of all the user defined table names
    in a database or all the rows returned by a SELECT statement

Cursors are often used to provide a scrolling capability
    This allows the batch to retrieve:

the next row	FETCH NEXT
the prior row	FETCH PRIOR
the last row	FETCH LAST
the first row	FETCH FIRST
the nth row	FETCH [ABSOLUTE | RELATIVE] n

Rows are processed individually on the server

Two SQL Server based implementations of cursors are provided by

1   the preferred method, which is ANSI SQL cursors that
    supports only single row processing
    Each 'fetch' will return only 1 row from the ResultSet

2   the procedural based method called engine cursors
    used by DB Library and ODBC cursor APIs
    (For a discussion of cursors see Cliff's WOSSA II Study Toolkit)

Cursors enable operations to be performed:
- *individual row operations*
- *operations on the entire ResultSet*

14.2A ANSI Cursors

can:
- process one row at a time
- Be used in triggers and stored procedures (row by row)

14.2B Enhanced SQL Engine Cursors

can:
- allow set-orientated processing
- be used with DB_Library and ODBC

14.2C ANSI SQL Cursors

Statement	Description
DECLARE	Creates & defines a cursor
OPEN	Opens a declared cursor
FETCH	Retrieves a row
CLOSE	Closes the cursor
DEALLOCATE	Removes the cursor definition

Example:
Cursors are best understood if you can look at a complete syntax of their use. This example establishes a cursor, populates it with the names of the tables that
have indexes and then prints the list

```
CREATE PROCEDURE sproc_indexes
AS
BEGIN
SET NOCOUNT ON
DECLARE tnames_cursor CURSOR
FOR
        SELECT  name
        FROM    sysobjects o
        WHERE   type = 'U'
        AND EXISTS
            (SELECT *
            FROM   sysindexes I
            WHERE      i.id = o.id
            AND    indid BETWEEN 1 AND 250)
        ORDER BY name
FOR READ ONLY

DECLARE @table_name varchar(30)
OPEN tnames_cursor
WHILE (1=1)
        BEGIN
                FETCH NEXT FROM tnames_cursor INTO @table_name
                IF NOT @@FETCH_STATUS = 0
                    BREAK
                DECLARE @cmd varchar(255)
                SELECT @cmd = "EXEC sproc_ind " + @table_name
                PRINT ' '
                PRINT  @table_name
                EXEC (@cmd)
        END
CLOSE tnames_cursor
DEALLOCATE tnames_cursor
END
```

Note: the DECLARE, OPEN, FETCH, CLOSE and DEALLOCATE in bold

14.2C.1 DECLARE statement

The DECLARE statement creates and defines the attributes of
the cursor
(variables in the SELECT statement are evaluated at this time)

There are 2 types of cursor:

 1 INSENSITIVE

 allows only row operations from the cursor ResultSet
 creates a temporary table for the ResultSet as a snapshot
 of the data - obviously the data is not updatable

 2 SCROLL
 allows all methods of fetching

 If you use the keyword SCROLL you can use FETCH to
 move forward and backwards (and to absolute positions)
 within the ResultSet

Syntax:

**DECLARE cursor_name [INSENSITIVE | SCROLL] CURSOR
FOR select_statement
{FOR {READ ONLY | UPDATE [OF column_list]}}**

Example:

**DECLARE authors_cursor CURSOR
FOR
  SELECT   *
  FROM authors**

The syntax detail will be discussed later
If neither READ ONLY nor UPDATE is specified then:

- *If ORDER BY or INSENSITIVE is specified in the SELECT
  statement then the cursor is READ ONLY*

- *If GROUP BY, UNION, DISTINCT or HAVING are specified
  in the SELECT statement then the cursor is READ ONLY
  and INSENSITIVE*

14.2C.2   OPEN statement

Opens the cursor (and creates a temporary table if necessary)

Both: the SELECT criteria and
                 the Ordering criteria
       are fixed when the cursor is opened

Syntax:

   OPEN cursor_name

Example:

   OPEN authors_cursor

After a cursor has been opened use the global variable
       @@CURSOR_ROWS to receive the number of
       selected rows in the cursor

If the number of rows expected in the ResultSet is large
       SQL Server may choose to populate the KeySet
       asynchronously on a separate thread. This allows fetches
       immediately even if the KeySet is not fully populated

   The configuration option cursor_threshold (in sp_configure)
   is used to set the threshold at which SQL Server will generate
   KeySets asynchronously

The @@CURSOR_ROWS variable returns one of:

-m   the cursor has been populated asynchronously
      the value of m is the number of rows in the KeySet

n   n refers to the number of rows

0   No cursor is open

Cursors defined without the INSENSITIVE option are referred to as Keyse

   When you open such a cursor the server executes the SELECT
   statement to fix both the Membership and the Order
       of the ResultSet cursor

   DELETE and UPDATE (which deletes and appends) will
       leave holes in the cursor since the cursor operates against
       the fixed Membership and Order in the ResultSet
       You have to close and reopen the cursor to refresh the
       Membership and Order of the ResultSet

Rows that have been deleted will appear with all NULLS in variable columns and spaces in char columns and default or zero values in the other NON NULL columns

When a cursor is opened the row pointer is above the first row and has to be moved to the first row by using FETCH

14.2C.3 FETCH statement

Retrieves a specific row from the cursor

Syntax:

```
FETCH
    [NEXT]
    [PRIOR]
    [FIRST]
    [LAST]
    [ABSOLUTE n]
    [RELATIVE n]
[FROM] cursor_name
[INTO @variable_name . . .list]
```

Example:

```
FETCH NEXT
FROM authors_cursor
```

A global variable @@FETCH_STATUS, will be updated at each EXECution of FETCH, having the following values:

0   successful FETCH
-1 No data because the requested cursor position exceeded the ResultSet
-2 The row returned has been deleted after the cursor was opened

Always use this variable to determine the validity of the data returned from a cursor fetch before attempting operations

14.2C.4 CLOSE statement

Closes an open cursor

Syntax:
> CLOSE cursor_name

Cursors use resources

Some cursors hold locks

CLOSE leaves the datastructure ready for reopening
> but releases memory held for buffering

When you finish working with a cursor, close it
> then do end of process programming

When you reopen a cursor the row pointer returns to the top
> of the RowSet

14.2C.5 DEALLOCATE

The cursor optimization plan takes space in memory

When you de-allocate a cursor you have to re-declare before you can reopen it

When you de-allocate you release its datastructure
> and removes the definition of the cursor

Syntax:
> DEALLOCATE cursor_name

14.2D When to use Cursors

The book "SQL Server Unleashed" gives this bit of advice:

In general, avoid cursors
If you can't, then avoid scrolling cursors
If you can't avoid using EXEC statements, do variable driven absolute addressing in the cursor

As a general guideline, it is better to perform row level processing on the client instead of the server because client resources are cheaper

When to use Cursors

Use ANSI SQL cursors to perform row by row logic in stored procedures

Use Engine cursors:

- * to fill list boxes or grid on a large ResultSet
- for ad hoc applications in which the ResultSet is unknown and potentially large
- when multiple active ResultSets are needed in one transaction (connection)

When not to use cursors

ANSI SQL cursors should be avoided if row by row logic can be performed by a SQL set operation

Engine-side (Server) cursors should be avoided to:

- perform batch processing that retrieve the entire ResultSet
- retrieve a small ResultSet that can be cached on the client
- perform procedural logic that could be performed in a stored procedure

Lightning Source UK Ltd.
Milton Keynes UK
UKOW03f1936210115

244867UK00006B/224/P